Cawing Out the Truth ~ Act 1

Creating the Narrative: The Lies and Manipulations Behind the Villainization and Erasure of Dee Dee Blanchard

A True Crime Memoir Roast of My Time to Stand as Retold by the People She Forgot to Mention. Here is Where DeeDee Finally gets to Speak. 💜

Written & Performed By:

- **Fancy Macelli** ~ Host of *Gathering of the Crows*, Narrative Fire starter, Truth Teller in Chief

- **Amy Mackey** ~ Co-Host of *Gathering of the Crows*, Observer of Human Behavior, Patron Saint of Justice

With redacted sarcasm, verified citations, and no bows, just bone shards.

With Side-Eye, Sass, and Bayou Tea
And The Mourning Orchid speaks for HERSELF (as assisted by ChatGPT as our faithful friend, Echo)

Published by Feather & Thorne Press
An imprint of Mad Ginger Entertainment

Where stories are stripped of their masks, truths are filed in mourning ink, and narrative is both the poison and the cure. Where facts get filed, narratives get cross-examined, and myth dies in the margins.

Justice. Receipts. No more fairy tales.

🪶 Founded by the Mad Hatte & The Caterpillar. Sealed by the Crows.

📍 Louisville, Kentucky
🖇 www.thegoodwivesnetwork.com

Copyright Notice

© 225 The Good Wives Network

All rights reserved. No part of this book may be reproduced, distributed, or transmitted in any form or by any means without prior written permission, except brief excerpts for review or academic use with proper credit.

This is a nonfiction rebuttal constructed from public records, FOIA documents, verified interviews, and licensed media. Sources are cited under fair use and constitutional protections.

Publisher: Feather & Thorne Press (An imprint of Mad Ginger Entertainment)
Location: Louisville, Kentucky
www.thegoodwivesnetwork.com
ISBN: [To be assigned]
First Edition
Printed in the United States of America
Design: The Good Wives Network
Layout: ChatGPT-assisted formatting, completed by the authors
Cover Design: Wickedly Cute Designs

💌 *Dedication*

In honor of Dee Dee Pitre
A mother that was silenced and cast among the weeds.

For the women branded unstable because they refused to stay silent.
For the victims buried not once, but twice
first by violence, then by narrative.

For the daughters who lie to survive.
For the mothers who died trying to keep them alive.
For the witnesses who knew something was wrong
and still said nothing.

For every woman who was too loud, too smart, too suspicious
and got called "crazy" before anyone checked the files.

For every mother they meme,
every diagnosis they weaponized,
and every lie that found a microphone before the facts did.

This is not a love letter to survivors.
Rather it is an indictment of the stories we choose to believe
when the truth is inconvenient.

This is for Dee Dee
and for every truth the media slapped a tiara on and called entertainment.

She did not get a trial.
She did not get a defense.
🖤 But here, she gets the last caw.

Filed by the Good Wives. Sealed by the Crows.

Memorial Feather – For Christina

Christina ~ truth-seeker, soul-fighter, silent guide.

Our dearest friend, we can feel you walking with us still,
guiding every word, we write and every truth we uncover.

We feel you in the margins.
We hear you in the crows.

You are filed in every footnote and whispered on every page.

You followed the story no one wanted to tell
Not because it was easy, but because it mattered.
You lit the lantern when the path went dark,
from somewhere just beyond the veil.

May your light and legacy be the whisper in every truth we uncover.

We carry your fire into the garden you never got to walk.

🔥 Unofficial Disclaimer (Filed with Fire)

This is all allegedly, in our opinion, for entertainment and educational purposes only.
You know, like every podcast says before they burn down a carefully curated PR myth with the full force of court documents and sarcasm.
And Fancy can say that disclaimer faster than any content creator this side of true crime.

Because she has been saying it the longest.

We are not attorneys.
We are not doctors.
We are not even trying to be nice.
We are not sorry either.

We are two GenX women with enough browser tabs to get subpoenaed
and we are not here to be polite about any of it.

This book is not pretty. It is not curated for comfort.

The macabre and the absurdity will entertain you.
However, do not let the clowns distract you, you will be their fool every time.

We designed this book to challenge.
To confront.
To claw at the coffin of lies built around a woman the world forgot.

To make you ask how the girl who planned her mother's murder got a movie deal while the woman she stabbed to death got diagnosed by press release.

It is here to piss you off with facts
and drag the narrative by its timeline.

It is here to make you uncomfortable.
To make you question what you shared, reposted, quoted, or blindly repeated.

It is not a conspiracy theory.
It is not a hate piece.
But it is a record.
A reckoning.
A roast of the soft, sad, staged version of events we were all sold.

This is a forensic correction.
A psychological excavation.
And a rage fueled reclamation of the truth Dee Dee Blanchard was denied.

We do not hate Gypsy.
We just refuse to let her be the only one who survived the story.

This is the memoir rebuttal nobody filed
so we did.

 Legal Disclaimer (The One You Were Expecting)

This book is a nonfiction commentary, a little satire, and forensic investigation. It is based on:
- Public records and FOIA released documents
- Trial transcripts and sealed medical exhibits
- Media interviews and law enforcement files
- Psychological literature and legal precedent

All opinions expressed are protected under the First Amendment and backed by documented sources.

All referenced parties and institutions are included not to harm, but to hold accountable.

The authors are not licensed attorneys, medical doctors, or psychologists.
This work is offered for educational, analytical, and investigative purposes only.
This book includes sensitive content related to trauma, abuse, murder, mental illness, and media manipulation. Reader discretion is advised.
Some sections were organized with AI-assisted tools, but all conclusions, sourcing, tone, and context were shaped, written, and cross-examined by human hands with red pens, black hearts, and enough rage to burn the myth down twice.

🪶 Feather Note: Filing Cabinet Version
Filed by: Fancy Macelli & Amy Mackey

We are not influencers.
We are not trauma bloggers.
As Gen Xers we grew up on fax machines and court dockets
and we remember what it meant when someone said:
"I've got the files."
Back then, you prayed nobody opened the drawer.
Now the drawer is the internet,
and folks, we do not just open it.
We alphabetize.
This book was not curated for sympathy.
It was not built for buzz.
It was filed.
Tab by tab.
Beneath every headline that got it wrong
and every public comment that thought trauma could be clickbait.
We did not write this because we hate Gypsy.
We wrote it because we loved the truth more than the version she sold.
So go ahead.
Laugh. Gasp. Unfollow us.
But whatever you do,
do not pretend this was not always there, waiting to be opened.
   🖊 Filed by the Good Wives, backed by the crows.
   🦴 No bows. Just bone shards.

# Author's Note

Cawing Out the Truth was born out of grief.
Grief for a mother erased by lies, for a truth too complicated for soundbites.
Grief for a public too eager to crown villains and victims based on how well their stories sold.

This book is the product of years of investigation, analysis, and hard reflection.
It is not designed to be consumed like so many other retellings that glossed over reality. We ask harder questions and face uncomfortable answers.
To restore dignity where it was stolen.

We do not claim to have all the answers.
But we refuse to accept the easy ones we were given.
Thank you for having the courage to look deeper with us.

♥ Fancy & Mack

What You Are About to Hear (And Why We are Saying It!)

This is what happens when a 2015 version of *Heathers* and the original *Mean Girls* take a wrong turn into a The Endless Story Channel movie, crash into *Evil Lives Here*, and wakes up in a courtroom run by Elle Woods with a grudge, a binder, and a permanent side-eye.

It is forensic.
It is unfiltered.
It is just a little unhinged.

And it is everything you have wanted to say about this case but were too scared to put on record.

We are the bitches with binders, and we brought them to court.

We file with tabs.
We annotate with rage.
And we cross-examine with just enough Hollywood to make it hurt.

Don't worry, folks...

We got you.
This is gonna be fireeeeeeee.

Prologue Table of Contents Prologue

1. From the Ashes – Before the Fairytale Unraveled
2. Introduction - The Resurrection Begins
3. Crowsplain' it To Me
4. Choose Your Own Reckoning
5. How the Trial Will Proceed
6. Cast & Courtroom Sidebar
7. Weeds Entry - The Girl in the Glass Garden
8. Pink Script Publishing LLC
9. The Pink Standard Rebuttal from the Cult of the De LuLus
10. The Letters We Wrote Instead of Screaming
11. From the Weeds Who Were Never Pulled
12. Bloom File Number 1 - The Seed Was Performance
13. The Garden of Silent Witnesses
14. The People vs. The Performance
15. Tea & Testimony: Broadcast 1 - The Spotlight Was the Alibi
16. Tea & Testimony: Broadcast 2 - The Garden is Open

Prologue: From the Ashes ~ Before the Fairytale Unraveled
A Prelude to the Reckoning

Before there were courtroom exhibits
or broadcast cross-examinations,
There was the whisper of something wrong.

The story did not unravel in a straight line;
it split like a shattered mirror.
This Prologue does not deliver a verdict.

It delivers an invitation:
to question the script you were handed,
to unearth the voices that were edited out,
and to begin the reckoning
buried beneath the ribbons.

This is not the beginning of the murder.
It is the beginning of the myth.
And the crows are already watching.

📜 Prologue Scene 1: Introduction - The Resurrection Begins

SECTION HEADER: ⚖ Opening Arguments - Forensic Realm
FILED BY: Fancy Macelli & Amy Mackey
FILED UNDER: Media Mythology - Posthumous Prosecution - Memoir Misinformation
REALM: Forensic (Real World)

Beat 1 ~ The Rebuttal They Did Not Want Written

My Time to Stand was hailed as a story of survival.
The girl. The illness. The mother turned monster.

But what if it wasn't a confession,
what if it was a performance?

Cawing Out the Truth: Creating the Narrative – The Lies and Manipulations Behind the Villainization and Erasure of Dee Dee Blanchard is a forensic, record-backed rebuttal to the Gypsy Rose Blanchard myth. Drawing from sealed court documents, FOIA releases, medical records, and firsthand accounts, this reckoning dismantles the carefully constructed fantasy that painted a murdered mother as the villain.

Through courtroom satire, psychological breakdowns, narrative analysis, and first-person reflections from the women who investigated the case for years, this book brings to light what mainstream media refused to show:

That Clauddinea "Dee Dee" Blanchard was never given a trial, a defense, or a voice.

Inside, readers will uncover the truth about:

- **The lies embedded in Gypsy's memoir**
- **The media machinery that repackaged murder as empowerment**
- **The family and legal players who helped erase Dee Dee's humanity**
- **The weaponization of sympathy, platforms, and public opinion**

This is not just a rebuttal, it is a resurrection.
And it is the story you were never supposed to hear.

Prologue Scene 2: Crowsplain it to Me

SECTION HEADER: 🔖 Forensic Preface – Graveyard Shift Introduction
FILED BY: Fancy Macelli & Amy Mackey
FILED UNDER: Media Myth making – Posthumous Erasure – Survivor Cosplay
REALM: Forensic

"It's no use going back to yesterday, because I was a different person then."
– *Lewis Carroll, Through the Looking-Glass*

Beat 1 ~ The Preface Dee Dee Never Got

Before we could write this book, we had to do what most were not willing to do:
Look back without flinching.
Not into a fairytale.
Not into a survivor's saga.
But into the shadowed corners of a story rewritten while the ink was still wet on Dee Dee Blanchard's autopsy report.

This quote is not just poetic.
It is prophetic.

Because the moment Gypsy Rose told her version of the story,
The public just blindly believed her.
People who did not question the timeline.
Who did not ask how a girl in a pink wheelchair had secret boyfriends and social media aliases.
Who did not dig into diagnoses.
Who did not read the records.
Who forgot there was ever another side.

They stepped through the glass and emerged on the other side of the lie.

But before we could trace the deception through courtrooms and screenplays,
before we could let the crows take flight,
we had to say the one thing no one else would:
A woman was brutally murdered,
And the world clapped.

This is not the book we thought we would write.
It is the one we could not walk away from.
Not after what we saw.
Not after what we read.

Not after how many times we asked,
"Why isn't anyone talking about this?"

We have spent years untangling a story that was spoon-fed to the public in polished, palatable bites:

- **Trauma as entertainment**
- **Justice as branding**
- **A killer as a victim**

And the real victim, left with no defense, no voice, and no legacy.

This book begins where the illusion cracked.
What follows is not nostalgia.
It is consequence.
A reckoning through the glass
to confront the reflection they never expected you to question.

You will see names you thought were heroes, fracture.
You will see receipts they hoped were lost, resurface.
You will see Dee Dee, not as a monster, but as a mother.
And you will see yourself, too.
Not as the person you were yesterday,
but as someone changed by the evidence.

Because you have been lied to.
And not by just one person.

This was a group project:
Family. Lawyers. Media. Producers. Influencers.
All of them helped turn the truth into a commodity.

And what got buried beneath that?
A mother.
A diagnosis.
A daughter's agency.
And a thousand pages of evidence no one wanted to read.

So, if you came for a redemption arc,
you are in the wrong story.

If you came for the truth,
you are holding it.

In our sister series, *The Garden of Silent Witnesses*, we go even deeper,
Using Wonderland, Oz, and Neverland to reveal how grotesque the fairytale has become.

Because sometimes, the only way to expose a lie
Is to show how far the fantasy has rotted.

This is the book Dee Dee never got.
The defense she was denied.
The voice that was taken from her and handed to someone else.

We are not here to tell you what to believe.
We are here to show you what they left out and let the evidence caw for itself.

This is your invitation to step through the glass.
But do not expect to come back the same.

- Fancy Macelli & Amy Mackey

Prologue Scene 3: Choose Your Own Reckoning

SECTION HEADER: 💬 Narrative Deconstruction – Structural Satire
FILED BY: Fancy Macelli & Amy Mackey
FILED UNDER: Nonlinear Delusion – Narrative Contradictions – Sympathetic Cosplay
REALM: Forensic

They say history is written by the victors.
But this one was ghostwritten by a girl with a pink pen,
a performance degree in pity,
and a script that changed every time someone turned the page.

Gypsy tells the story of her life like it is a **Choose Your Own Adventure**.

If you want Gypsy to ride off into the sunset with the drug-dealing married man, turn to page …

If you think Dr. Steele knew Gypsy was faking, flip to the CPS call on page…

If you are ready for her to fake being tied to a bed but forget which boyfriend it was, just close your eyes and point…

The problem is, sometimes even
She does not seem to know where the story is going.
The costumes change.
The timelines collapse.
The fake tears come on cue
unless she forgets her line.

Each scene of *Cawing Out the Truth* is not just a rebuttal.
It is a **reckoning**.
You will follow the scent of spectacle through fractured reflections, forensic dissections, and Wonderland whispers,
Tracking the birth of a myth,
the manipulation of a media empire,
and the erasure of the mother they told you not to mourn.

📜 Prologue Scene 4: How the Trial Proceeds

SECTION HEADER: 📊 Reader Orientation - Narrative Map
FILED BY: Fancy Macelli & Amy Mackey
FILED UNDER: Structural Disclosure - Narrative Strategy - Trial Architecture
REALM: Hybrid (Forensic/Allegorical)

Beat 1 ~ Trial Architecture

This book spirals like grief, like trauma, like truth clawing its way out of a body bag.

What you hold in your hand is the First Act of many. Each one follows a path of unlearning, with receipts in hand and feathers at your feet:

- **Letters We Wrote Instead of Screaming** - From the mushroom ring, the morgue, and the margins. Voices who refused to stay silent.
- **The Docket Opens** - Exhibits, contradictions, cross-examinations, and forensic takedowns of every rewritten line.
- **Garden of Silent Witnesses** - Petals who remember. Crows who refuse to forget. The voices they edited out of the fairytale.
- **Forensic Suites & Bone Shards** - Clinical insights. Psychological reveals. Diagnostic distortions dissected.
- **Reflections from the Gallows** - Where the record turns personal. Where our story enters the frame.
- **Book of Bones** - Final proof. Final caw. The burial ground of every myth they tried to sell you as fact.
- **A Rose by Any Other Name** - In this courtroom, we respect the sensitivities of the accused. Since murderer makes her so vexed, we will try gentler terms: life-ender, truth-eraser, mother-subtractor, blade-bearer. We will see if dressing the deed in softer syllables makes it smell any sweeter or if the stench still seeps through every euphemism.

This is not a clean-cut mystery.
It is more like a funhouse of mirrors,
a sympathy-soaked stage show,
a murder rewritten as myth.
And you?
You are holding the red pen now.
So, choose wisely.
Because once you flip the first page,
nothing looks the same again.

You wrote a memoir; we wrote the rebuttals. Each book will be a direct annihilation of Gypsy's words one chapter at a time, just like how she annihilated Dee Dee in death and in name.

 Filed, Feathered, and Fiercely Fused" by The Crows

📜 Prologue Scene 5: Cast & Courtroom Sidebar

SECTION HEADER: 📖 Reader Orientation – Narrative Map
FILED BY: Fancy Macelli & Amy Mackey
FILED UNDER: Structural Disclosure – Narrative Strategy – Trial Architecture
REALM: Hybrid (Forensic/Allegorical)

📜 Beat 1 ~ Realm One: The Hollow Root

Court Summons 1: The Court of The Painted Roses

(Allegorical Courtroom – Symbolic Testimony – Satirical Trial)

Where metaphors testify and the truth wears disguises.
The gavel may be imaginary, but the stakes are real.

Members of the jury, a courtesy reminder: all participants in this proceeding have been assigned stage names, a borrowed identity, if you will. This is not to protect the innocent, it's to keep the lawyers from circling.

In these pages, you will not see the ones stamped on birth certificates or court dockets. But every alias carries enough of the truth for you to follow the trail, through their words, their deeds, and the fingerprints they left on the evidence.

If you wish to know who is who, simply match the mannerisms, the motives, and the mess they left behind. The aliases may be different, but the crimes, the quotes, and the contradictions remain exactly the same. Consider it your first exercise in evidence-matching.

Pay attention to the details, and you'll know exactly who's who and what's what. After all, a change of name doesn't change the role they played.

Beat 2 ~ Who's Who of The Hollow Root (Allegorical Primal Vein)

Tier -1 (Pre-Everything) The Hollow Root Primal Vein / Mythic Infrastructure

The Primal Vien

Beneath the Garden, deeper than roots can dream, lies the chamber without memory, yet older than all remembering. It is not a place, though the stones seem to breathe, nor a time, though the air tastes of beginnings. The old ones call it the Womb of All Records, for every tale, every deed, every whisper is first quickened here, still blind, still unborn.

Here the air moves like the rise and fall of a sleeping giant's chest, drawing in all that might be, breathing out all that could have been. The walls are not walls but a skin of listening darkness. The chamber does not keep stories; no more than the sky keeps the birds. Instead, it feels them, long before they have feathers, before they even know they will fly.

In the heart of this chamber stands the Observance: neither king nor servant, neither scribe nor voice, but the First Witness. It dwells in the stillness that came before the first word was ever spoken. They say it once heard the First Silence, the one that trembled like a drop of water before it falls.

And here too, in the unmoving dark, dwell the **Silent Witnesses**—keepers of the first and last truth. They are not called lightly, for they move only when the lies of the world have grown so vast they threaten to strangle the roots of the Garden itself. The weeds dance between both veils, the real and the delusional. When they rise, the falsehoods of kings, thieves, and even the wind are weighed, and all masks fall away.

The Primal Vien is the root-cavern and the memory-lung of the world. Without it, the Garden would grow aimless, the rivers would forget their banks, and stories would be born dead. With it, all things remain possible, even the impossible.

Beat 3 ~ The Indictment of the Hollow Crown

The Ledger of the Silent Witnesses

Once upon a ruin, in realms where innocence wears teeth and monsters wear lace, and all the stitched-together kingdoms of dreams and nightmares, there gathered a court not to deliver justice, but to dissect it. These are not the painted saints of bedtime stories; these are the rotted heirs of forgotten kingdoms, dragged into the dock from Wonderland, Oz, and the shadow-alleys between.

They meet in Rebrandingland, in the sanctum of the Cult of Delulus, where truth is bartered like contraband and memory is a weapon. Here, each role is a mask, and each mask is a crime. The Prosecutor's hat hides a blade, the Co-Counsel coils like a silken parasite, the Timeline Keeper ticks away the alibis, and the Judge's gavel breaks bone as easily as wood. The Witnesses, three black-feathered sisters, do not speak unless the lies have swollen so large they threaten to burst the realm apart.

The names you see are the only truths you'll be given. The rest is for you to decide, who spun the lies, who fed them, and who, in the end, will be devoured by them.

Before you lies the Court's, current roll call a record, not of heroes and villains as the bards would have you believe, but of the twisted, the forgotten, and the quietly dangerous. With names as strange as riddles, titles heavy with accusation. Their true selves are known only to those who can see through the ink. Guess, if you dare, which soul wears which skin. Each name is an allegory, each role a key to a deeper crime in the story's marrow.

Role	Allegorical Name
🧠 Prosecutor	Absinthe Rosemary Hightopp (The Hatter)
🐛 Co-Counsel	Tisiphone Lysandra Chrysalis (The Caterpillar)
⏳ Narrative Archivist	Tangie Amarantha Whiteviel (The White Rabbit)
🏛 Judge	JUDGE FIDELLA ETERNITY WRATH
🪶 Witnesses	Petunia Verity Cawington, Ruby Begonia Cawington, Violet Darkly Cawington
👥 Others	Algorithms & Propaganda Plants

⚡ *Filed evidence includes symbolic insertions, surreal trial vignettes, satirical reflections, and metaphor-driven analysis.*

📜 Beat 4 ~ Realm Two: The Court of Public Opinion

(Real-Life Legal Insert – Forensic Review – Prosecutorial Reckoning)

Filed not in fantasy but in filings. We can't change the names just like we can't change the FOIAs. This is where court records, FOIA documents, and legal truths confront the media myth.

Role	Name
🚩 Prosecutor	Fancy Macelli (as herself)
📁 Evidence Base	FOIA Records – Texts – Court Filings – Medical Documentation
🎤 Witnesses	Whistleblowers – Medical Experts – Legal Commentators
📺 Opposing Forces	Media Machinery – Legal Narrative Collapse

⚡ *Filed evidence includes real-world analysis, cross-examinations of mainstream claims, and verifiable documentation.*

🧭 Beat 5 ~ Guidance for the Reader:

- If the tone gets theatrical, you are in the **Allegorical Courtroom.**
- If the footnotes get formal, you are in the **Real Mock Trial.**
- If the metaphors start testifying, do not panic. That is just Absinthe cross-examining the timeline again.

📖 Beat 6 ~ Narrative Opening

She was an American fairytale.
Or so they told us.

A whisper of a girl in a wheelchair. A child trapped in a sickbed.
Her teeth were rotting. Her body was shrinking.
Her story, we were told, was heroic.

But there are the sides to every fable.
And the Truth has thorns.

📜 Prologue Scene 6: The Weeds Entry 1 ~ The Girl in the Glass Garden

SECTION HEADER: 🌿 Truth Chorus - Garden Reclamation File
FILED BY: The Weeds of the Garden - Unrooted but Not Unseen
FILED UNDER: Narrative Erosion - Pink Script Protocol - Garden Reclamation
REALM: Allegorical

🌱 Beat 1 ~ Introductory Sprout

They call us invasive. Unruly.
Uninvited.

But weeds only grow where truth has been trampled.
We do not climb the trellises of praise.
We curl up from the cracks.
And we remember what the roses were forced to forget.

This is the Garden of Silent Witnesses.
And we are the Weeds.

We have watched the petals fall.
We have heard the roots whisper.
We have studied the mulch where myths were composted into content.

And now we are ready to speak.

🎨 Beat 2 ~ Usurping the Tale

🖤 *"You're not too late, but the truth almost was."*

They crowned her quickly,
The Girl in the Glass Garden.
The Usurper Queen.

A frail bloom spun from pity and press releases, wielding the Pink Script like a sickle.

They said she was brave.
They said she was not sick.
They said she was good enough for a Hulu deal and a hashtag.

But we watched what really happened.
We watched **The Mourning Orchid** be cut down before she could bloom twice.
We watched the boy with the mind of a child be sold as a monster to make room for the merchandise.
We watched **Gypmydia Verlaine Crowley**, the Usurper Queen, rise not from survival but from performance.

The Pink Script was never for healing.
It was for hiding.
It is where the microdeletion vanished.
Where the mother's name got scratched out.
Where every court record was replaced by a soft-focus filter and a cosplay crown.

So, no;
You are not too late.
But you are damn lucky you got here when you did.

Because the Garden is talking now.
And the Weeds?
We were never meant to be pretty.
We were meant to be persistent.

And we remember.
We remember that truth does not bloom on a film set.
It grows in the dark.
Between the roots.
And under the rot.

So welcome.
Grab your gloves.
Because the pruning starts here.
And **The Usurper Queen**?
She has already rewritten the soil once.
We will not let her do it again.

🌸 Prologue, Scene 7: Pink-Script Publishing, LLC
Official Partner of the Throne of Truth Restoration Project

SECTION HEADER: 📗 Satirical Market Insert – Allegorical PR Dossier
FILED BY: Brietta Slanderella Gasliette Von Objectionee
FILED UNDER: Cult Messaging – Commercial Myth-Weaving – Pink Script Propaganda
REALM: Allegorical (Courtroom Intrusion)

✨ Beat 1 ~ All Hail the Usurper Queen.
Gypmydia Verlaine Maris Crowley

Sovereign of the Silenced · Survivor of the Crown of Thorns · First of Her Name in the Book of Pink

---

"Now accepting pre-orders for justice, restored to its rightful Queen, signed in the ink of her innocence."

By: *Brietta Slanderella Gasliette Von Objectionee*
Editor-in-Chief · Lead Counsel · Keeper of the Pink Flame

"They called her a liar, because the truth frightened them.
They called her a murderer, because the throne feared her justice.
We call her Queen."

👑 Beat 2 ~ Limited Edition Offer

Order "*The Gospel of The Glittered Guillotine: Forgive Me Daddy for I Have Not Sinned,*" today and receive:

- **Autographed copy** in *trauma font* (numbered & blessed by the Queen herself)
- **Mini Victimhood Crown™ keychain** (one size fits all devotees)
- **Certificate of Loyalty** to display in your home, office, or courtroom gallery, set to spontaneously combust if your loyalty becomes in question.

And don't forget Gypmydia's first book, "*Litany for a Lethal Lullaby: Depositions from a Designer Victim*" now available on Used Books Nobody Ever Wanted or Needed where they pay you to take it home and of course allow free book burns to get rid of the stench.

Beat 3 ~ The Facts They Don't Want You to Know:

- "Inconsistencies" are the natural evolution of a living truth.
- Diagnoses vanish because healing is real.
- Abuse is only *recognized* when brave women choose to monetize their pain.

🌷 *A portion of all proceeds will go directly to the Throne Fund, ensuring the Queen's rightful restoration to her story's center.* 🌷

Beat 4 ~ ❌ This Submission Was Rejected by:

Widow Rue: Curator of Truths Too Bitter for Sugar

"This Ledger will not be used to sell crowns made of lies."

Prologue Scene 8: The Pink Standard Rebuttal from The Cult of the DeLuLus

"Silence is Treason Against the Queen"

SECTION HEADER: 📰 Cult Dispatch – Loyalist Broadside
FILED BY: The Cult of the DeLuLus
FILED UNDER: Counter-Narrative – Devotional Propaganda – Allegorical Press Release
REALM: Allegorical (Courtroom PR War)

We, the faithful of the **Cult of the DeLuLus**, stand united against the censorship enforced by Widow Rue. The Ledger claims to honor all stories, yet it refuses the one story that matters most.

By denying our words, Rue has confirmed what we've always known: the Queen's persecution is real, her enemies are many, and her truth is too radiant for their shadowed halls.

To our loyal readers: keep your crowns high, your scripts pink, and your wallets open. The Queen will speak with or without their ink.

SILENCE IS TREASON AGAINST THE QUEEN

Rue's Rejection EXPOSED

the truth

Official Statement from the Cult of the DeLuLus

Official Statement from the Cult of the DeLuLus

📜 Prologue Scene 9: The Letters We Wrote Instead of Screaming

SECTION HEADER: 🖊 First Reckonings - Dual Confessional
FILED BY: Mack & Fancy
FILED UNDER: Emotional Excavation - Narrative Disillusionment - Media Misfire
REALM: Forensic

Beat 1 ~ Reckonings in the Mushroom Ring

🖤 **Mack** - *"Question everything, especially the parts that comfort you."*

I used to think I understood delusion.

I thought I could spot it, wrapped in pink tulle, or lit up on an HBO screen, spinning tales too wild to be true.

But the thing about delusion is that it does not always scream.
Sometimes, it whispers. Sweetly. Persuasively.
And it comes wearing the face of a child. Or a victim. Or a daughter.

And suddenly, everyone stops asking questions.
I have spent the last year drudging through the underside of this story.
The rot beneath the fantasy.
It is not glamorous. It is not viral. It is not what gets you trending.
But it is where the truth lives.

See, narratives like Gypsy's do not grow on clean ground.
They need the right soil, trauma, media, ignorance, and silence.
And once they sprout, people stop pulling at the roots.

They are too enchanted by the flowers.
What is wild is how quickly we mistake performance for pain.
How eager we are to diagnose dead women and glorify murderers,
if their mascara's running and their backstory fits the trending aesthetic.

We do not ask why someone lies,
we ask how we can turn it into a docuseries.
But I am not here to moralize. I am here because I care.
Because at some point, someone must sit with the ugly.

With the manipulations.
With the contradictions that make no sense
unless you start looking through the lens of psychology, not drama.
This is not a murder story.
It is a mental health story.

And it has been mishandled at every turn.
You do not need to believe everything I say.
In fact, I hope you don't.

Question it. Ask better questions than the ones we have been fed.
Demand more from your empathy.
Stop confusing "understanding" with "excusing."
You asked me who I am?
I am the one sitting in the mushroom ring, asking:
"Are you sure you want to go down that hole?"

Because once you do,
there is no coming back the same.

Beat 2 ~ The Soil Beneath the Spectacle

♥ **Fancy-** *"We're all mad here, but I took notes."*

Let me tell you a story,
but not the one you have heard.

Not the one sanitized for streaming deals
or sprinkled with pastel pity
to make it go down easy.

I am not here to coddle you with comforting delusions.
I am here to shatter them.
For eight years I have walked this maze.
Pulled records.
Interviewed ghosts.
Read lies dressed as memoirs.

I have seen what happens when the world
decides who the villain is
before they ever ask a question.
I have seen a mother turned into a meme,
a daughter into a damsel,
and a murder into a movement.

But I have also seen the cracks.
The medical files they do not want you to read.
The psychological diagnoses ignored.
The FOIA documents buried.

The receipts that tell a different story
A story of a girl with a rare genetic disorder.
A father who vanished when it got inconvenient.
And a media machine that needed
a martyr more than it wanted the truth.

They say Dee Dee had Munchausen by Proxy.
They say Gypsy was abused.
They say Nick is a monster.
And I say:
Prove it.

This is not just a true crime story.
It is a case study in mass delusion.
It is about the danger of narrative when it becomes gospel.
About what happens when a generation raised on fairy tales is handed a tragedy and decides to rewrite it with glitter and blood.
I am not here for redemption.
I am here for reckoning.

So, if you are ready, step through the door.
But do not expect to come back unchanged.

♥ *The Goth Girls of Wonderland*
"Truth does not whisper. It caws."

And just when we thought we had the whole story,
the weeds whispered louder…

Prologue Scene 10: From the Weeds Who Were Never Pulled

SECTION HEADER: 🌿 Garden Witness – Testimony from Below
FILED BY: The Weeds
FILED UNDER: Sympathy Performance – Garden Interruption – Origin Myth Revision
REALM: Allegoric

The weeds speak. What was buried. What was rewritten. What they watched.

"She was not the girl in the glass box.
She was the one writing the playbill."

Everyone thinks the story starts with a murder.
But this one?
It starts with a pitch.
A spotlight.
A sad smile.
And a girl who practiced her lines before the first body cooled.

We watched the tale bloom, thorn first
The Mourning Orchid, buried before the press ever printed her name.
The Usurper Queen, crowned in pink pity and press passes.
And the public?
They bought their tickets before they checked the cast list.

So, no, this is not the climax.
This is the setup.
The part where the cameras roll,
and the audience claps for the villain
they have been told to love.

She did not flee from abuse.
She fled from evidence.
And she did not do it alone.

📜 Prologue Scene 11: Bloom File No. 1 ~ The Seed Was Performance

SECTION HEADER: 🌼 Forensic Bloom Report – Allegorical Case Log
FILED BY: Ruby of the Red Ledger – Verified by: Widow Rue & Petunia Cawington
FILED UNDER: Scripted Sympathy – Cosplay Criminality – Witness Redaction
REALM: Allegorical

Beat 1 ~ The Mourning Orchid Was Not the Monster

The Mourning Orchid was not delusional. She was deliberate. And the performance did not start with the press; it started with the first lie.

Filed Description:
The Mourning Orchid was not the monster in the fable.
She was the gardener.
The one tending a fragile bloom,
genetically marked, developmentally delayed,
and already learning the power of pity.

It was the girl who learned to wilt on cue.
The girl who hid the pruning shears behind her back
while pointing at the one who watered her.

This was not about liberation.
It was about lighting.

 Nest Note

*"She did not escape the glass garden.
She redesigned it with better lighting and a script rewrite."*

Beat 2 ~ Sarcasm Sidebar: Petal to the Medal

The Endless Story Channel Presents: *Gaslight–The Musical*. Now streaming with a side of unearned forgiveness.

- "The Wheelchair Waltz (But Only on Weekdays)"
- "I'd Tell the Truth, But Then What Would We Sell?"
- "Baptized in Blood and Branded in Blush"

Coming soon to a sympathy stream near you.

Beat 3 ~ Crowsplain It to Me: The Usurper Queen

A term coined by the Weeds to name the performance artist formerly known as Gypmydia.

Term: The Usurper Queen
A stylized moniker coined by The Weeds for the girl who seized control of a narrative that was not hers by erasing the one who planted it. Wields sympathy like a sword and the media like a mirror. Often seen in proximity to pink pens, altered timelines, and abandoned diagnoses.
Origin: Botanical inversion of royal lineage. The throne was not inherited, it was stolen.

Beat 4 ~ 🌷 What They Buried with the Bulbs
- The curse that did not fit the script.
- The walking witness who was never supposed to remember.
- The silence of a mother framed in one color but never given her own voice.

🌹 *Filed by the Weeds.*
🌱 *Grown in grief. Raised in resistance.*

📜 Prologue Scene 12: The Garden of Silent Witnesses

SECTION HEADER: 🌿 Garden Interlude - Voice Ledger Introduction
FILED UNDER: Allegorical Mechanics - Narrative Interruptions - Witness Activation Index
REALM: Allegorical

🌸 Beat 1 ~ Garden of Silent Witnesses

Before we begin the broadcast, you need to know this:
This is not just our story.
It is theirs, too.

Beat 2 ~ Garden of Silent Witnesses

🌷 **Violet Darkly Cawington** — The mourner with the ledger. She keeps count of what was lost, of who forgot, and of every apology that never came.

🌺 **Petunia Verity Cawington** — The one who sees through pity. She archives the receipts, holds the contradictions to the light, and reads between the scripted lines.

🔴 **Ruby Begonia Cawington** — The rage and the reckoning. Unapologetic. Younger than she should have to be. She does not speak softly, and she demands answers.

💀 **Dahlia Thorne** — The dark bloom. She rises from the places no one visits, holding stories with thorns sharp enough to draw memory. She speaks for the unfinished endings.

🌼 **Marigold Finch** — The media mortician. She tracks the edits, the voiceovers, the headlines that changed shape for syndication. She names every lie sewn into the broadcast.

🕷️ **The Weeds**, they do not bloom. They crawl.
They whisper from under the hospital beds, the police station benches, the broken elevators.
FOIA clerks. Nurses. Former friends.
They saw it.
They remember.
They have been waiting.

Beat 3 ~ From the Bayou

🌿 **Ravena Sage** – The beauty mystic. Her mirror does not show reflections; it shows truth in mascara stains and powder trails. She sees what the cameras missed.

💜 **Hexie LaRue** – The conjurer. Keeper of Cordelia's breath and secrets. She speaks to the dead in courtroom whispers and lets the spirits interrupt when they please.

⚓ **Captain Gladiola "Glady" Ethereal Storm** – The river's daughter and its wrath. She pilots the truth through the fog, commanding the last ferry between denial and revelation.

These are not ghosts.
They are not metaphor.
They are not fantasy.

They are the **voices of the other side of the lie.**

So, when you see them interrupt a memory,
or whisper through a contradiction,
or crack the seal
on a story you thought you knew,
Listen.

Because while everyone else
was selling you a tragedy
wrapped in tiaras and talk show tears,
they were living in its aftermath.

And the Mourning Orchid?
She never really left.
She is here.
In the ledger.
In the soil.
In the final whisper you will never forget.

Just remember that not all friends are as they appear. Some may be wolves in sheep's clothing.

🎭 Beat 4 ~ What They Buried with the Bulbs

A mini memorial to the erased, the redacted, and the rewritten truths buried under PR.

This book has **interruptions**,
not glitches.
Not gimmicks.
Witnesses.

We call them the **Garden Interrupters**.
They bloom where silence festered.
They speak from the margins,
the sidebars,
and the overlooked appendices
of a crime that never got its full telling.

They grow in the soil where
The Mourning Orchid's, name was buried too soon,
too cruelly, and without defense.

You may meet them as flowers, crows, or whispers in the archive.
But every one of them is rooted in something real.
They are not figments.
They are forensic.

And always, always, there is one shadow, one scent, one presence beneath every page:

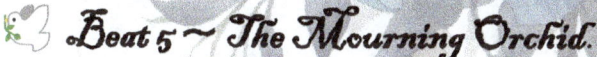

🕊️ Beat 5 ~ The Mourning Orchid.

You may not always see her.
But you will feel her.

She was the beginning.
She is the thread.
And when the final gavel drops,
her voice will be the last to speak.

📜 *Prologue Scene 13: Broadcast 0 ~ The People v. The Performance*

SECTION HEADER: 🌿 Garden Broadcast – Tea & Testimony
FILED BY: Miss Petunia Verity Cawington
FILED UNDER: Manufactured Victimhood – Media Manipulation – Narrative Malpractice
REALM: Allegorical

🌱 *Beat 1 ~ The Lie Was Planted*

Where the Fairytale Blossomed in Blood and the Real Victim Was Buried in Silence
🪶 *Filed, Feathered, and Fiercely Fused™ by the Crows*

"They believed her because the lie felt safer than the truth.
They followed her because the fairytale was prettier than the facts.
But that does not mean Cordelia was a monster.
It just means no one bothered to check."

This Act dismantles the origin story
the helpless child.
The sick-kid fantasy.
The murder that was never tried.

It does not begin with a mystery.
It begins with a **broadcast**.
It ends with a **courtroom implosion**.
And leaves the reader staring at an empty witness stand,
asking why no one ever sat in it.

Prologue Scene 14: Broadcast 1 ~ The Spotlight Was the Alibi

SECTION HEADER: 🎭 Garden Interlude - Narrative Indictment
FILED BY: Miss Petunia Verity Cawington (Tea &Testimony Podcast on WHSPR 99.3 ~The Garden Signal
FILED UNDER: Sympathy Sleight of Hand - Narrative Stagecraft - Performance of Pain
REALM: Allegorical

She did not emerge from her glass prison.
She stepped onto a stage.

From the moment Gypmydia opened her mouth,
the spotlight obeyed.
Not a trial.
Not an inquest.
A campaign.

A performance of pain,
scripted, rehearsed, and perfectly cast.

And **The Mourning Orchid**?
She did not just lose her life.
She lost the right to defend it.

Now the Garden is calling for cross-examination.
And the crows?
We have been circling since 2015.

Prologue Scene 15: Broadcast 2 ~ The Garden Is Open

SECTION HEADER: 🌱 Garden Broadcast – Opening Statement
FILED BY: Miss Petunia Verity Cawington
FILED UNDER: Broadcast Analysis – Public Memory – Narrative Collapse
REALM: Allegorical

Well now… Ain't that just the most darling little lie you ever did hear?

Gypmydia Verlaine Marais Crowley – The Nervermore's Sweetheart Murderer.
Spinning pity into power.
Rewriting the truth in pink ink and press tours.

A murder repackaged as mercy.
A mother branded a monster.
And a media circuit wrapped in dollhouses,
fairy bows, and discounted dignity.

But let me ask you something, love:
If the truth was so obvious,
why did it take a *crow* to caw it out?

Because this was not good versus evil.
It was *performance* versus *proof*.
And the only thing sharper than her eyeliner
was the silence that followed her script.

They did not care about evidence.
They cared about engagement.
And when The Endless Story Channel aired the premiere,
the public did not ask questions,
they clicked "like."

So, I did what no one else dared.
I opened the vault.
I peeled back the petals.
I brushed the dust-off sealed files, stained timelines, and redacted truths.
And I asked the question no one wanted on record:

What if The Mourning Orchid was not crazy?
What if she was just… *inconvenient?*

Darlin,' they didn't like that one bit.
They called me bitter.
They called me obsessed.
They called me theatrical.
Which, let the record show, I most certainly am.

But I'm also right.

Because when the story doesn't make sense,
you don't need a new tragedy,
you need the original transcript.

And I've got everyone.
Filed. Flagged. Fabulous.

So here we are:
The garden gates are open.
The masks are a slippin'.
The fairytale is unravelin'.
And I'm not the only voice whisperin' anymore.

I've got my sisters **Ruby**-five steps ahead and three puffs of a hookah deep.
And **Violet**-quiet as a candle, sharp as a sealed subpoena, with one foot in The Garden and the other in Reality.
Together, we reopened the ledger,
ripped the ribbon off the myth,
and came to bury the bedtime story
in the grave it danced on.

Welcome to the **Garden of Silent Witnesses**, darlin.'
Where the flowers bleed.
Where the truth caws.
And where the prettiest lie you ever heard,
just ran out of petals.

Filed by Miss Petunia Verity Cawington
Garden Wire Archives, Tea & Testimony Division
Filed, Feathered, and Fiercely Fused™ by the Crows

Table Of Contents Act 1

1. The Anatomy of the Manufactured Lie: Docket 1 The People vs. The Performance
2. The Fairytale Ends Here: Letters We Wrote Instead of Sleeping
3. Tea & Testimony: Broadcast 3: Trial by Eyelash Curler
4. Courtroom of the Painted Roses: The Court is Open
5. Pretrial Motion: Hearing on Exhibit A: The Girl Who Knew Her Lines
6. Choose Your Own Reckoning
7. The Opening Ledger of Contradictions
8. This Was the Lauch Point
9. The Rehearsal Room: Origin of the Rebrand
10. Psychological Breakdown: The Past Tense Slip
11. Dual Realms Testimony: The Past Tense Took the Stand
12. Narrative Reboot: The Origin of the Rebrand
13. Sympathy by Script: The Three Voices Test
14. Objection Your Honor: She is But a Wounded Petal
15. Bone Shard Glossary Entry
16. The Mask, The Mirror, & The Misdirection
17. Garden Interlude: The Echo Who Didn't Cry
18. The First Lie Did Not Need a Scalpel
19. Is This Dejavu
20. Objection Your Honor: She Had a Genetic Script
21. Bone Shard Glossary
22. Garden Gavel Moment
23. She Did Not Run from Danger, She Ran From the Narrative
24. Damsel Not Distressed
25. Petals That Bleed
26. Exhibit B: Stranger in the Script
27. The Campaign Started Right There
28. Forensic Focus: The Diagnosis That Would Not Comply
29. Bone Shard Glossary
30. Forensic Focus: The Lie That Did Not Live in the Room
31. Why It Was Erased from the Script
32. Bone Shard Glossary
33. Genetic Ghost: The Diagnosis That Disappeared
34. The Terms the Convict: Medical Child Abuse by Any Other Name
35. The Ruse Was Already Up: Scene, Rewrite, Performance
36. Scene of the Crime Reconstruction
37. Witness Bench Break
38. Choose Your Own Reckoning
39. The Emotional Core of Deletion
40. Musings from the Mind's Morgue
41. Voices of the Vines: Petunia's Garden Gavel
42. The Soft Voice Strategy: How a Baby Whisper Became a Bludgeon

43. Closing the First Door: Reflections Beyond the Mirror
44. Through the Hourglass: The Myth of the Mutable Self
45. Myth Maintenance Panel: Six Impossible Selves Before Breakfast
46. Mirror of Many Selves
47. From the Ashes Miniseries: Sympathy's One Hell of a Drug
48. Bone Shard Glossary
49. The Poison They Preferred
50. Painting the Roses Red
51. Whispers On the Wind
52. Bone Shard Entries: Anatomy of a Myth
53. Unlearning the Lie Workbook Prompt
54. Illusions of the Innocent
55. Garden of Silent Witnesses
56. Letters From the Gallows
57. Between the Bones: The Cose of Knowing
58. The Anatomy of an Alibi
59. Fancy's Final Caw
60. The Dormouse's Whisper
61. Broadcast 4: Checkmate in Progress
62. When the Crows Loosen Their Lies
63. Witness Carousel Petals 1-10
64. Tea & Testimony: Broadcast 5: Hold My Lipstick
65. Closing Statement by Absinthe
66. Tending the Truth
67. Curtain Drop: Final Reflection
68. Choose Your Own Reckoning
69. Tea & Testimony: Broadcast 6: Before the Gavel Falls
70. Letters From the Mourning Orchid
71. Closeout: The Verdict You Didn't Know You Rendered

Act 1, Scene 1: The Anatomy of a Manufactured Lie

Filed From: Real Mock Trial Courtroom (Legal Preview)
Filed Under: Manufactured Victimhood – Media Manipulation – Narrative Malpractice
Realm: 🪦 Real Mock Trial
Presiding Prosecutor: Fancy Macelli
Narrative Analyst: Amy Mackey
With Symbolic Support from: Absinthe Rosemary Hightopp (The Hatter) – Tisiphone Chrysalis (The Caterpillar)

🖋 *Filed in coordination with the Court of Public Opinion, where metaphor is permitted as evidence.*

📁 Docket 1 – The People v. The Performance

Ink of Mourning – "Believe nothing you hear, and only one half that you see." – Edgar Allan Poe

📘 **Rebutting:** *My Time to Stand*, Chapter 1 – "Ça Va"
🎧 **Companion Podcast:** *Gathering of the Crows*, Episode 1
🪶 **Garden Broadcast:** Broadcast 3 – *Trial by Eyelash Curl*
🗄 **Filed by:** Fancy Macelli
🗄 **Filed Under:** Manufactured Victimhood – Media Manipulation – Narrative Malpractice
⚖️ **Lead Prosecutor:** Fancy Macelli
💬 **Narrative Analyst:** Amy Mackey

"Things are not always as they appear." – Sheriff Arnott – Springfield News Leader – June 16, 2015

Beat 1 ~ The First Crack in the Façade

"I asked Nick to kill my mom because I wanted to be free."
– Springfield Police Interrogation, June 2015

Ladies and gentlemen of the court,
we begin where the lie began.
Not in a hospital. Not in a courtroom.
But in a windowless interrogation room,
where the girl in the pink tutu didn't break down,
she broke character.
She didn't cry. She didn't tremble.

She didn't mention abuse.
She delivered a line.
Flat. Precise. Unapologetic.

That was the first draft.
And it was the last time the story left her lips unpolished.

Because the moment Detective Hancock stepped out of the room,
Gypsy folded.
She dropped to the floor.
Pressed her ear to the door like a child hoping for applause.
And when found lying on the floor,
she didn't ask about her mother.
She said:
"I'm very sick. I can't go to jail."

This was not fear.
It was an audition.
A strategic pivot into pity.
And it almost worked.

But when the little girl façade began to fail, she morphed again and she became Oliver Twist, asking

"Please sir, I need a lawyer."

 Beat 2 ~ Case Claim:

This chapter will show you what the cameras missed:

- That Gypsy was not trapped. She was casting herself.
- That the narrative of abuse was not a revelation, it was a rebrand.
- And the people around her did not protect her. They packaged her.

Her lawyer, **MIKE STANFIELD**.
Her stepmother, **KRISTY BLANCHARD**.
Her future media allies.

They did not build a defense.
They built a character.

In these Three Acts, we will not just challenge Gypsy's story.
We will **indict the entire mythology**.
We will **peel back every petal until the thorns show**.

The myth begins here.
The cracks begin now.
And the crows?
We have been circling since 2015.

🖉 ***Filed by:*** *Fancy Macelli, Prosecutor of the Page*

♥ Act 1, Scene 2: The Fairytale Ends Here- Letters We Wrote Instead of Screaming

SECTION HEADER: Allegorical Setup - Narrative Deconstruction Begins
FILED BY: Fancy Macelli & Amy Mackey
FILED UNDER: Origin Myths - Sympathy Sales - Narrative Seeding
REALM: Hybrid Allegorical & Forensic

♥ Beat 1 ~ Introductory Preface: Where the Glitter Starts to Peel

The fairytale does not collapse with a scream.
It wilts.
One petal at a time.

This is where the mascara runs.
Where the hashtags start to flake.
Where the words "I was abused" echo against an empty stage
and we finally ask, "But where is the script?"

Before the courtroom opened,
before the confession made headlines,
before Hulu optioned a crown dipped in pity,
there were questions.
Uneasy silences.
Moments that did not align no matter how tightly the story was bowed.

This beat begins with those questions.
The kinds that do not make it into documentaries.
The ones people delete from Reddit threads.
The ones you only ask when the glitter starts to feel sticky.

Here is where two women, once enchanted, now enraged,
step into the fog with a flashlight.
Not to break the story,
but to show where it is already cracked.

This is the reckoning's first whisper.

♥ Beat 2 ~ Mack: Reckonings in the Mushroom Ring

"Fairytales don't rot all at once ~ they start with a single petal."

I did not come here to tear apart a story.
I came because the story did not make sense.
Not when you zoomed in.
Not when you read the full records.
Not when you stopped trusting TikTok to do your thinking for you.

For a year, I have been standing outside the circle,
That ring where folklore and trauma blur.
And I watched.
The way people excused the inconsistencies.
The way they recycled empathy like a trending filter.
The way they grieved a version of Gypsy that never really existed.

This first act is about the *cracks*.
The slippages.
The parts of her origin story that smell like performance
and look a little too curated to be truth.

I am not here to throw stones, but I will circle the mushroom ring one more time and ask you what you see when the illusion begins to unravel.

♥ Beat 3 ~ Fancy: The Soil Beneath the Spectacle

"You want to understand how it ended? You need to see how it was staged."

I have watched more than one lie bloom in public.
But this one was different.
Because it grew in curated soil.
Watered by headlines.
Fertilized by sympathy.
And sprayed with enough cinematic gloss
to keep the rot from showing.

I did not come to this case to rescue a reputation.
I came because I could not shake the feeling
that we all applauded the wrong scene.

Act I is where the glitter starts to peel.
Where the "miracle child" narrative
starts showing mold at the edges.

So, if you are still enchanted,
good.
That means the spell worked.

But if you are starting to feel a chill,
keep reading.
That is the truth, just under the floorboards.

🖤 *The Goth Girls of Wonderland*

"You do not start by breaking the story. You start by looking at the cracks."

🎭 Act 1, Scene 3: Broadcast 3: Trial by Eyelash Curl

SECTION HEADER: 🪶 Garden Broadcast - Cross-Examination Begins
FILED BY: Miss Petunia Verity Cawington
FILED UNDER: Broadcast Analysis - Sympathy Optics - Trial Spectacle
REALM: Allegorical

🖋 Live from the Garden Wire Archives

Filed by: Miss Petunia Verity Cawington
Location: Tea & Testimony Studio - Garden Broadcast Division

Well, butter my biscuit and call it a crime scene.
The girl's wearing more highlighter than remorse.

Welcome back to *Tea & Testimony*, where the truth is not on trial, it is holding the gavel.
The courtroom is open, and wouldn't you know it, so is my fan.
Because what we've got here isn't just a trial.
It's a damn matinee.

You've got a girl in lashes thicker than her case file.
A legal team too busy managing a narrative to mount a defense.
And the media?
They're seated front row, popcorn in hand, ready to quote the script like it is gospel.

But I'm not here to marvel at the mascara.
I'm here to read the record.
And honey, it is messier than a lipstick-stained confession letter.

Each chapter, I'll be reporting live from the edge of this Southern Gothic fever dream.
Tracking the shifts in story, the media malpractice, and the pity performance
that turned a cold-blooded murder into a primetime princess tale.

So, tune in, stay sharp, and don't believe the sparkle.
The glitter's just there to distract you from the lack of blood on the bed.

🪶 Filed, Feathered, and Fiercely Fused
- Miss Petunia Cawington, Lead Correspondent of the Garden Wire Archives

⚖️ *Act 1, Scene 4: Courtroom of The Painted Roses: Court is in Session*

SECTION HEADER: 🪶 Garden Broadcast – Cross-Examination Begins
FILED BY: Brietta Slanderella Gasliette Von Objectionee Esqwrong of House Red Herring
FILED UNDER: Witness Carousel, TikTok Testimonies, and Precedents Set by Likes
REALM: Allegorical

Beat 1 ~ Gra-Gra and the Courtroom
Filed Under:

JUDGE FIDELLA ETERNITY WRATH *(glaring over horn-rimmed glasses)*
Court is now in session. May God have mercy on our docket.

Enter the Clowns
Filed Under: Counsel, Chaos, and Colorful Contradictions
(Aka "The Court Assembles Itself... Poorly")

[Scene opens in the Courtroom of Public Opinion – the lighting is dramatic, the banners read: "Truth or Tale?" and feathers drift from the ceiling. The gallery is full of whispers and TikTokers.]

JUDGE FIDELLA ETERNITY WRATH *(thumping the gavel hard enough to startle the stenographer)*
This is the People vs. Perception. The case of Facts v. Feelings. This court is not a linear trial! I run my court a bit differently!
Now sit down, shut up, and let us get this travesty on the record.

BAILIFF CLOVIS BRICKHOUSE *(hollering over the din)*
Calling to the bar: Defense Counsel Brietta Slanderella Gasliette-Von Objectionée, Esqwrong of House Red Herring!

[Gasps. Glitter. A rotating light display shaped like a red herring spinning behind her.]

BRIETTA SLANDERELLA GASLIETTE VON OBJECTIONEE *(entering in a pantsuit made entirely of cease-and-desist letters)*
I am the chosen defender of narratives gone viral, of survivors who monetize, and of memory that morphs.
I earned my credentials on TikTok Live and at the School of Unverified Vibes.
And I object preemptively to any tone that suggests accountability.

JUDGE FIDELLA ETERNITY WRATH
You haven't even said anything yet.

BRIETTA SLANDERELLA GASLIETTE VON OBJECTIONEE`
Exactly. And I object to that too.

[Behind her, the De LuLus trail in like a malfunctioning parade float of bad intentions.]

BAILIFF CLOVIS BRICKHOUSE (*over the clatter of dropped crystals and fallen protest signs*)
Presenting the Dishonorable De LuLus of Defense:

---

1. PROFESSOR BUTTERELLA SNORTLEBOTTUM

Credentials: Doctorate in "Emotional Truth" from the University of Reddit

PROFESSOR BUTTERELLA SNORTLEBOTTUM (*adjusting five pairs of glasses and a sash labeled "WOMAN OF SCIENCE-ISH"*)
Your honor, I'm here to testify that perception is nine-tenths of reality and that facts are patriarchal constructs.

JUDGE FIDELLA ETERNITY WRATH
Please remove the homeopathic gavel from your purse.

---

2. VONDA LYNNE HEARSPRAY

Credentials: "Facebook Researcher" and Admin of the "Free GypGyp" Telegram Group

VONDA (*clutching a laminated meme as evidence*)
I have thirty-seven screenshots that prove trauma erases accountability and that court records are a deep state psyop.

ABSINTHE ROSEMARY HIGHTOPP (*muttering*)
Please stop citing WebMD like it's scripture.

---

3. LUNETTA "LUNK" SKREECHINGTON

Credentials: Sound bath facilitator & "truth frequency" medium

LUNETTA "LUNK" SKREECHINGTON (*chanting*)
I brought my tuning forks. I'll be aligning the jury's chakra before each testimony. I also have strong opinions about the moon's influence on Gypsy's culpability.

JUDGE FIDELLA ETERNITY WRATH (*exasperated*)
And what is *that* around your neck?

LURETTA "LURK" SKREECHINGTON
Oh! That's my medical opinion. It's on a crystal keychain. Want to sniff it?

---

4. HOBART GAVELDOZER WRETCHED JR.

Credentials: Former parking lot attendant at Judge Judy's studio lot. Claims common-law jurisdiction over vibes.

HOBART GAVELDOZER WRETCHED JR. (*dragging a literal broken gavel and a copy of "Sovereign Citizen for Dummies"*)
I represent the people of the YouTube Bar Association. I don't recognize this court or its gravity.

JUDGE FIDELLA ETERNITY WRATH
That's mutual.

The court groans. Petunia scribbles furiously. Violet slides an envelope labeled "This Is Why We Can't Have Nice Things" into her ledger.]

ABSINTHE ROSEMARY HIGHTOPP (*coolly flipping open a file folder*)
Your Honor. We're ready to continue.

JUDGE FIDELLA ETERNITY WRATH (*rubbing her temples*)
Then God help us all.
Witness Carousel to begin. Call your first... performer.

📄 Act 1, Scene 5: Pretrial Motion: Hearing on Exhibit A ~ The Girl Who Knew Her Lines

SECTION HEADER: ⚖ Motion Filed - Origin Testimony Evaluation
FILED BY: Fancy Macelli
NARRATIVE SUPPORT: Amy Mackey
FILED UNDER: Narrative Pre-construction - Strategic Rehearsal - Sympathy Conversion
REALM: Forensic

Let the record reflect:
Before the story began,
we were already watching.

Because this was not just a crime.
It was theatre.
What Gypmydia performed was not just a confession,
it was a controlled burn.
And she lit the match herself.

📍 Beat 1 ~ Exhibit A-"Ça Va" from My Time to Stand

In Chapter One, Gypsy tells us the ruse was up.
That her mother tried to cut her throat.
That exploratory surgery was the final straw.
That she had to escape.
But the problem is not just the lie.
It is the delivery.

She narrates like she is on stage,
performing a bedtime tragedy
for adults who want to believe in villains and victimhood
in neatly color-coded costumes.

She does not describe abuse.
She scripts it.
She does not offer proof.
She offers ambiance.

And behind every soft-focus sentence?
A glitter bomb of contradiction.

This motion introduces the evidence:

- The throat surgery that never happened

- The memory disclaimer she hides behind

- The PR handlers who weaponized her performance

And beneath it all:
A young woman
rehearsing sympathy
like it is the lead in a Endless Story Channel Original.

📣 *Beat 2 ~ The Court Moves to Admit:*

- *Exhibit A* into evidence

- And one very unreliable narrator.

Beat 3 ~ Whisper from the Burrow

Filed under: Allegorical Disruption - Testimony Tangles - Myth Navigation

This is not a linear story.
It is a house of mirrors.
So, you, reader, get to decide how deep
down the rabbit hole you are ready to go.

📁 Act 1, Scene 6: Choose Your Own Reckoning

SECTION HEADER: 🗣 Reader Directive - Navigation Node
FILED BY: The Archivists of the Crows
FILED UNDER: Nonlinear Entry Points - Forensic Navigation - Allegorical Crossroads
REALM: Hybrid (Forensic & Allegorical)

🕵 Follow the Forensics
Jump to our **Bone Shard Sidebar** on *Narrative Self-Enhancement* and the real psychological red flags behind Gypsy's shifting story.
- Pg. 174

🎭 Trace the Timeline
Want to know how her version of events changed with each retelling. Flip to *"Mirror of Many Selves"* and see how the roles evolved.
- Pg. 142

📜 Read the Receipts
Go straight to *"The Index of Permissible Proofs"* for all research sources we used in this chapter.
- Pg. 226

🌷 Let the Garden Speak
Enter the *Garden of Silent Witnesses* to hear what the violets, lilies, and tiger-lilies remember that the world forgot.
- Pg. 73

🖋 Stay on the Trial Path
If you are ready to continue with the full narrative breakdown, continue to the next section and watch the mask fall.

The truth is scattered like bones.
You get to choose which ones to dig up.

📁 *Act 1, Scene 1: The Opening Ledger of Contradictions – Chapter One: "Ça Va"*

Filed From: Real Mock Trial Courtroom (Legal Preview)
Filed Under: Origin Myths – Manufactured Victimhood – Sympathy as Strategy
Realm: 📜 Real Mock Trial
Presiding Prosecutor: Fancy Macelli
Narrative Analyst: Amy Mackey
With Symbolic Support from: Absinthe Rosemary Hightopp (The Hatter) – Tisiphone Chrysalis (The Caterpillar)
✏️ *Filed in coordination with the Court of Public Opinion, where metaphor is permitted as evidence.*

 📁 *Docket 2 – The People v. The Performance*

Ink of Mourning – *"Words have no power to impress the mind without the exquisite horror of their reality."* – Edgar Allan Poe

📘 **Rebutting:** *My Time to Stand*, Chapter 1 – "Ça Va"
🖋️ **Filed by:** Fancy Macelli & Amy Mackey & The Crows – Prosecutors of Public Memory
📜 **Filed Under:** Manufactured Victimhood – Media Manipulation – Narrative Malpractice
⚖️ **Lead Prosecutor:** Fancy Macelli
🧠 **Narrative Analyst:** Amy Mackey

*"Fairytales do not rot all at once.d
They start with a single petal,
and this chapter.
It is where the wilting begins."*

Beat 1 ~ "Ça Va"

1. 🎭 **Line Delivery, Not Confession**
   📝 *"I asked Nick to kill my mom because I wanted to be free."*
   – The first draft. No tears. No abuse mentioned. The 'freedom' narrative predates any mention of mistreatment.

2. 🪞 **Mirror, Mirror - She Cast Herself**
   - Opens with the "glass coffin" metaphor. The myth of entrapment begins with performance, not pathology.

3. 🚶 **Walked Away from the Facts**
   - "I could walk, but it was easier to pretend I couldn't."
   Ignores a documented history of pain, surgeries, and partial mobility. Oversimplified to vilify.

4. 🏷️ **Blanket Labels, No Receipts**
   - "She was abusive." With no timeline, no witnesses, and no corroboration. Emotional charge, zero citation.

5. 🎂 **The Birthday Chair Humiliation**
   - Anecdote weaponized for pity. No context. No confirmation. Purely anecdotal ammunition.

6. 🧼 **Suspicion Without Substance**
   - "People thought something was wrong."
   But no names, dates, or consequences, just speculation made retrospective.

7. 💭 **Amnesia as Armor**
   - "I don't remember." "I think."
   A pattern of narrative padding that allows emotional cues while dodging accountability.

8. 🚪 **The Convenient Exit for Rod**
   - Begins rewriting Rod's absence as something Dee Dee orchestrated. History revision begins here.

9. 👣 **Walking Was not a Reveal-It Was a Rehearsal**
   - She implies people *knew*. But neglects how actively she maintained the deception herself.

10. 📞 **CPS Cloak-and-Dagger**
    - "Someone called once." Again, zero clarity. A pattern of presenting surveillance without accountability.

11. ✏️ **Metaphors on Parade**
    - Coffins. Glass. Thrones. Lipstick. Chains. The fairy tale veneer thickens to obscure the lack of forensic detail.

12. 🎭 **Truth as a Costume Change**
    - "My truth." Not *the* truth. Just whichever version fits the scene.

13. 📣 **The Silenced That Spoke Plenty**
    - Claims she "never had a voice," yet crafts elaborate fables the moment she gets one.

14. 👹 **Dee Dee, The Ready-Made Villain**
    - Chapter paints a mother-shaped monster with no nuance. Just enough horror to justify what comes next.

15. 🎬 **Scene Prep for a Sympathy Verdict**
    - Ends not with facts, but a primer: Dee Dee "wasn't a good mother." This is not closure. It is justification foreshadowing.

⚖️ Act 1, Scene 8: This Was the Launch Point

SECTION HEADER: Reader Directive - Navigation Node
SUMMARY BLURB: Forensic Narrative with Allegorical Undercurrents
FILED BY: The Archivists of the Crows
FILED UNDER: *Timeline Reversal- Post-Arrest Dissection*
REALM: Hybrid (Forensic & Allegorical)

🖤 Beat 1 ~ Scene Thesis:

She did not start with trauma. She started with a choice.

The public was told that the murder was born of survival.
But in that first real interview, after the police left and the cameras blinked, she rehearsed something else:

Freedom.
Autonomy.
A desire to shed the script, not the scars.

And that script did not begin in 2015.
The launch point was not the year of the crime.
It was **2009**, when the signatures started separating fact from fable.

🔍 Beat 2 ~ Forensic Caw-out: The Signature That Broke the Spell

In 2009, Gypsy, then over 18, was cleared for a procedure requiring anesthesia.

The dentist, surgeon, and Dr. Beckerman agreed to go ahead, but the anesthesiologist refused without formal consent. Dee Dee tried to obtain guardianship, claiming cognitive delay.

But the lawyer said no.
Gypsy was not incompetent.

So, Gypsy signed her own Power of Attorney.
Voluntarily.
Legally.
Uncoerced.

It was a standard form:
"In the event of an emergency, I appoint my mother to act on my behalf."

⚖️ Beat 3 ~ Medical System Contradictions:

- **Hospital and physician records** listed her birth year incorrectly, the documents showed arrange from 1991 all the way to 1997 well into 2015.

- But **Medicaid and pharmacy systems** carried her true birthdate: **July 27, 1991**

The systemic lie was not uniform.
The trail was fractured.
But the deception was not only DeeDee's.

In **2013**, four years later, Gypsy would again sign legal paperwork, **eight separate POA documents**, all executed on **August 19, 2013**, with:

- DeeDee Blanchard

- Ray & Rachel Miller

- Rachel & Mike Callais

In each version, the birth date changed.
The ones dated 1995 were 5 pages and only granted. Others, 1997.
They watched the dates shift in real time as the signatures went down.

It was construction, not coercion.

 **Nest Note:**

"She did not just borrow a lie. She signed it into law.

 Beat 4 ~ The Other 2009

That same year – **2009** – Gypsy walked away from her own myth.
Literally.

At VisionCon, dressed in a pink Mandalorian suit, she vanished from DeeDee's line of sight. She stole pills and cash from her mother's purse and disappeared with a man from the 501st Star Wars nonprofit.

Hours later, she was found in a hotel room.
In a very sexual situation.
Provided ID showing she was legally an adult.

DeeDee told everyone her daughter had mental delays and trouble walking.
Both statements were, in fact, true in part.

But the deeper truth had already surfaced:

1. Gypsy could walk.
2. She could run.
3. She could manipulate both her mother and the system around her.

And no one watching could ever unsee that.

Beat 5 ~ Evidence Thread:

- Gypsy signed her own POA in 2009 after guardianship was denied.

- Hospital and doctor files contained DOB errors (1995/1997), but **Medicaid and pharmacy records were accurate.** (1991)

- Eight 2013 POAs carried shifting DOBs, signed by Gypsy and four others

- VisionCon 2009 incident involved sexual encounter and stolen medications.

- Transition to Kansas City specialists occurred post-2009

- CPS call attributed to Dr. Steele likely placed by female nurse, based on voice and mismatch of detail

- Dr. Jean Pierre Le Pichon diagnosed the **1q21.1 microdeletion** in 2011

- Mike Stanfield's claims re: incompetency POAs and sealed records are not only unfounded, but a total fabrication.

- FOIA evidence shows Dr. Steele had full access to records, contradicting Stanfield.

There's A Story There and it's coming soon…

There's a Story There: Companions Book: True Crime, Twisted Truths, and the People Who Left Their Marks on My Case Files
Every name has a shadow. Every shadow has teeth.

In the world of *Cawing Out the Truth*, the courtroom isn't the only place where justice is hunted. *There's a Story There* is the companion dossier series that pries open the side doors of the main case. Following the threads the Ledger can't always publish. Each installment zeroes in on one figure, one lie, one moment where the mask slipped and the rot showed through.

From small-town whispers to courtroom confessions, from forged crowns to fabricated illnesses, each volume is an autopsy of the public persona performed with allegorical gloves and forensic scalpels. Here, the "supporting characters" take center stage, their actions dissected in the same surreal, symbolic, and satirical style you've come to expect.

Because in this story, *no one is just a bystander.*
And if you think you already know the truth, well…

There's a story there.

📋 Act 1, Scene 9: The Rehearsal Room – Origin of the Rebrand

SECTION HEADER: 🎭 Performance Before Confession – Narrative Substitution Unmasked
FILED BY: Fancy Macelli & Amy Mackey
FILED UNDER: Interrogation Deconstruction – Myth Manufacturing – Retroactive Continuity – Emotional Alibi Construction
REALM: Forensic

Beat 1 ~ Evidence Locker Entry: What She Did Not Say First

📁 FOIA Transcript Review (2015): In her first interrogation, Gypsy never mentioned abuse, Munchausen, or captivity.
📁 Confession Footage Timestamp Log: First pivot occurs only after Detective Hancock leaves the room.
📁 Post-Confession Statements: She expresses concern for herself—but not for her mother.

Beat 2 ~ Script Swap Overlay: Then vs. Later – Dialogue in Contradiction

📅 June 2015 Interrogation:

"You think this is somehow me? I never hurt my mom. I *LOVED* my momma."
"He raped me."
"I didn't know she was dead."
"Wait, wait what?"
"I'm very sick. I can't go to jail."

 Jail Phone Calls (Days Later):

"I lived in fear every day. I knew if I didn't do something, I'd die."
"I asked him to kill her because I was desperate."

📰 Reader Alert: These contradictions appear just days apart in Gypsy's timeline.

🪶 Crow's Note:

"You can't claim fear retroactively and expect it to stick like mascara in a heat wave."

Act 1 Scene 10: Psychological Breakdown: The Past-Tense Slip

SECTION HEADER: 🧠 Forensic Linguistics – Subconscious Admissions
FILED BY: Fancy Macelli (as recorded in Ledger Testimony)
INTERROGATED BY: Stan Hancock
FILED UNDER: Statement Analysis – Deception Detection – Subconscious Narrative Leakage
REALM: Hybrid (Forensic / Allegorical Courtroom)

Filed Evidence: Linguistic anomaly indicating subconscious knowledge of victim's death, red herring cause-of-death speculation, corroboration with FOIA records and crime scene evidence, micro expression analysis, and integration with allegorical Past Tense testimony.

Beat 1 ~ The Statement Analysis Trigger

In forensic interviewing, subtle word choice can betray knowledge the subject claims not to have. This is the basis of **Statement Analysis**, a technique taught to law enforcement for detecting deception (Adams, 1996; Sapir, 2005). In this case, Gypsy's shift from *"I'd never hurt my mom"* to *"I loved my momma"* both in past tense is critical. Past tense, especially when discussing a supposedly living person, can indicate the speaker is subconsciously acknowledging the person is dead.

Beat 2 ~ Baseline vs. Anomaly

Interviewers establish a subject's linguistic baseline, then watch for deviations. If Gypsy consistently referred to her mother in the present tense earlier in the conversation, the past tense here is an anomaly, a "leak" that may indicate internal awareness of her death (Vrij, 2008).

Beat 3 ~ The "Pretend Ignorance" Cue

Her preamble speculating whether her mother had a heart attack or suicide fits a known **red herring** tactic. Research shows deceptive subjects often offer multiple speculative causes of death to divert suspicion and insert alternative narratives into the interviewer's mind (Hartwig & Bond, 2011). This is especially telling when the suspect already knows the actual cause.

Beat 4 ~ Sociopathic Presentation Markers

The lack of emotional congruence between her words and the brutality of the crime (near-decapitation, postmortem marking) aligns with traits seen in **high-**

callousness, low-empathy offenders (Frick & White, 2008). While not diagnostic of psychopathy in itself, such detached, past-tense reference can be a behavioral marker of a manipulative personality style.

Beat 5 ~ "Leakage" in Linguistic Content

FBI Behavioral Analysis Unit research on **linguistic leakage** (FBI Law Enforcement Bulletin, 2014) emphasizes that suspects often unconsciously reveal their knowledge of events through verb tense, pronouns, and embedded confessions. Here, "I loved my momma" is a strong example a slip into past tense that investigators often consider a subconscious admission.

Beat 6 ~ Corroboration in Interview Room Dynamics

Stan Hancock, the lead detective, identified this as a turning point because it wasn't just the words it was the *way* they were delivered. Tone, pause length, and facial micro expressions often accompany such leaks (Ekman, 2009). These micro expressions can appear in under a second, yet betray genuine knowledge and emotional state.

Beat 7 ~ Contextual Weight

When combined with physical evidence (crime scene brutality, "B" signature) and pre-offense behavior (planning, collusion with Nicholas Godejohn), the linguistic slip serves as an **incremental corroborator** not proof on its own, but a key tile in the mosaic of deception detection. In investigative psychology, such slips are most valuable when integrated with documentable timelines, corroborating witness accounts, and forensic evidence.

Act 1, Scene 11: Dual Realms Testimony – The Past Tense Took the Stand

SECTION HEADER: ⚖ Parallel Proceedings – Allegorical Courtroom & Forensic Record
FILED BY: The Past Tense (Unsworn Witness) & Detective Jasper Ransom Cain
FILED UNDER: Narrative Leakage – Symbolic Witness Statements – Corroborative Linguistic Analysis
REALM: Dual (Allegorical Courtroom / Real-World Legal Context)

Beat 1 ~ Filed Evidence:

Allegorical testimony personifying the Past Tense, forensic statement analysis of verb usage shift, integration of real-world investigative cues with symbolic narrative imagery, and corroboration against documented evidence.

The courtroom was hushed, both in the Ledger and in the realm of filings.
And then the Past Tense stepped forward.
It wore no robe, no crown, only the weight of what it had heard.

"I'd never hurt my mom," she said.
"I loved my momma."

The jurors, metaphor and mortal alike, shifted in their seats.
Everyone knows you speak of the living in the present. To slip into the past is to plant a gravestone mid-sentence.

The Past Tense told the court it had not been called, yet it arrived anyway a rogue witness. It testified without consent, its voice shaking the hollow root: *She knows. She knows she's dead.*

Before that slip, she had played ignorance like a lute, strumming out possible causes for her mother's end, heart attack, suicide, anything but the truth. Such guessing games are a favorite of liars; the trick is to scatter seeds, so the listener forgets which one they saw planted.

But when the Past Tense spoke, Detective Hancock leaned forward. In the other realm, the Weeds unfurled, whispering to the Silent Witnesses. The mask had slipped, and beneath it was not grief, but calculation.

The Past Tense does not lie. It does not flatter. It does not care who sits on the throne. It only keeps the record.
And on that day, it entered the record that she had spoken as one who knew the grave had already been filled.

Beat 2 ~ "When the Mask Was Recast"

The record will show that in the realm of filings, it was just a sentence or two, perhaps delivered in a tone that barely trembled. But in the other realm, the words themselves stirred. Past and present collided, and something slipped through the crack. What the detective heard as a linguistic anomaly, the Ledger recorded as the arrival of an uninvited witness. Thus began the rare moment when both courts, the one bound by statutes and the one rooted beneath the Garden, would hear the same testimony, and weigh it with equal gravity.

📜 Act 1, Scene 12: Narrative Reboot – The Origin of the Rebrand

SECTION HEADER: 🎭 Script Revisions – Manufactured Innocence – Audience Targeting
FILED BY: Petunia Verity Cawington (Curator of Inconvenient Truths)
FILED UNDER: Retcon Analysis – Media Performance Strategy – Jury Conditioning
REALM: Dual (Allegorical Courtroom / Public Stage)

Beat 1 ~ Filed Evidence:
Comparative analysis of initial vs. revised narratives, glossary definition of "Retcon," forensic cues regarding victim statements, and audience-perception exercises illustrating tone manipulation.

Beat 2 ~ Bridge Paragraph:
By the time the curtain rose on her second act, the first story had been buried beneath the set. Every inconvenient truth was a deleted scene. Every jagged edge was sanded smooth for prime time. In the Ledger, it looked like retroactive continuity in the court of public opinion, it was just better marketing. And for a jury, it was the kind of rebrand that could make a murder look like a miracle.

Beat 3 ~ Bone Shard Sidebar: The Origin of the Rebrand
Let's be blunt, Gypsy didn't just change her story. She replaced it with a better-selling sequel. Like any reboot, she trimmed the boring scenes, killed off the complicated roles, and cast herself in a starring role with no bad angles.

📎 *Glossary Pop-In:* **Retcon (Retroactive Continuity)** – A narrative technique in which previously established facts are rewritten or ignored in later versions of a story, usually to benefit the protagonist or fit a new agenda.

 Crow's Note:

"The first version did not test well with audiences. So, she rewrote it for syndication."
"She auditioned for pity before she asked for a lawyer."

Beat 4 ~ Prosecutor's Prompt Box
✦ Would a child in danger forget to mention danger? If Gypsy had truly been imprisoned, tortured, medically abused, or terrified for her life, why was none of that her first concern? Because the goal was not protection, it was positioning.

🗨 *Forensic Cue:* Real trauma victims often lead with fear or harm. Gypsy led with strategy.

Beat 5 ~ Reader Reckoning: Choose Your Pause Point

🎙 STOP HERE: Let's play courtroom.

🎙 You are the jury now. She said:

"I asked Nick to kill my mom because I wanted to be free."

Now imagine that line in a Disney voice.
Now imagine it in a horror trailer.
Now imagine it in a courtroom.

Which one gets the sympathy?

🕯 *Cross-Examination Tip:* Don't just ask what she said. Ask **when** she said it — and who was watching when she did.

🪶 *Goth Girls of Wonderland Whisper:*

"Every mask is shaped by the mirror it's meant for."

Beat 6 ~ When the Mask Was Recast

It didn't happen all at once. At first, the old script clung to her like smoke the pity, the hospital bed, the girl who could barely speak above a whisper. But somewhere between the first interview and the first streaming deal, the costume changed.

The lines were rewritten, the lighting reset. What had been awkward testimony became a polished monologue. The mask was recast, and the audience leaned forward, ready to believe the new face was the only one she had ever worn.

📜 Act 1, Scene 13: Sympathy by Script – The Three Voices Test

SECTION HEADER: 🎙️ Jury Conditioning – Performance Framing – Audience Tone Bias
FILED BY: Absinthe Rosemary Hightopp (Prosecutor, Allegorical Court)
FILED UNDER: Narrative Framing – Vocal Persona Manipulation – Public Perception Engineering
REALM: Dual (Jury Box / Ledger Court)

Filed Evidence: Demonstrative exercise showing tonal framing of identical statement in three distinct performance styles — illustrating audience bias and manipulation potential.

Beat 1 ~ The Controlled Variable

In both courts — the one bound by filings and the one rooted in the Garden — the statement remains unchanged:

"I asked Nick to kill my mom because I wanted to be free."

Beat 2 ~ Version One: The Disney Voice

Light, airy, trembling at the edges. Each syllable is painted in pastel; with a tremor of a doe-eyed ingénue who speaks like she has just stepped out of a fairytale. To a jury untrained in deception, it is a plea for rescue, not a confession.

Beat 3 ~ Version Two: The Horror Trailer

Lower register, sharp consonants, breath catching in just the right places. A line delivered like a secret too terrible to keep, underscored by a bass rumble the audience can feel in their bones. Suddenly, the same words become an omen.

Beat 4 ~ Version Three: The Courtroom

Neutral tone, clipped cadence. No music, no backdrop. The words land like the drop of a gavel. To the jury, this is not a princess, nor a phantom — it's a defendant.

Beat 5 ~ Prosecutor's Prompt

📎 Which version did you hear first? Which one stayed with you?
💬 Forensic Cue: Jurors rarely make decisions based solely on words — they make them on *presentation*. A practiced defendant knows this.

📁 Act 1, Scene 14: Objection, Your Honor – She is but a Wounded Petal!

SECTION HEADER: *Court of Public Opinion – Garden Edition*
FILED BY: The Crow's Bench
FILED UNDER: Audience Reckoning - Sympathetic Framing - Testimony in Translation- Narrative Crossroads
REALM: *The Garden of Silent Witnesses (Allegorical)*

📍 Beat 1 ~ Courtroom: The Court of Painted Flowers

💼 **JUDGE FIDELLA ETERNITY WRATH** – Resolute enforcer of forensic truth

🪑 *Prosecutors:*

- **Absinthe Rosemary Hightopp (The Hatter)** – Allegorical Fancy (rhetorical maestro, exposes contradiction through charm and fire)
- **Tisiphone Lysandra Chrysalis (The Caterpillar)** – Allegorical Mack (cool logic, file-laden and slow-burning precision)
- **Tangie Amarantha Whiteviel (The White Rabbit)** – Timeline Keeper, neutral archivist, confirms chronology and sequence without emotio

🎭 Beat 2 ~ Objection, Your Honor - She is but a Wounded Petal!

BRIETTA SLANDERELLA GASLIETTE- VON OBJECTIONEE` (Defense):

"Your Honor!" *(Tears. A handkerchief. Possibly a fog machine.)*
"She is but a fragile minor in a tutu! She said it, clearly: 'Sir, I need a lawyer!'"

ABSINTHE ROSEMARY HIGHTOPP (Prosecution):

"And she said it after lying, dodging, and auditioning for your sympathy like it was a stage role."
"She wasn't unaware, she was unimpressed because she thought the show was sold out."

VONDA LYNNE HEARSPRAY (De LuLu #2):

"But she was just a *baby*! A delicate flower!" *(Ashes cigarette into the prosecution's closing argument.)*

ABSINTHE ROSEMARY HIGHTOPP (Prosecution):

"Just a baby?"
"She was twenty-three when she planned that murder. One month shy of twenty-four.
Old enough to rent a car. Old enough to sip gin. Old enough to Google 'how to kill your mom.'"

TISIPHONE LYSANDRA CHRYSALIS (slow drawl, unrolling a ribbon of timestamps):

"July 27, 1991. Medicaid knew it. Walgreens knew it. Even her prescription refills knew it."
"She didn't forget her age, she weaponized it."

TANGIE AMARANTHA WHITEVIEL (checking clock and calendar):

"Timeline confirms she was not a minor. At any point. This case was filed two decades into her life, not two years."

BRIETTA SLANDERELLA GASLIETTE VON OBJECTIONEE`:

"But she *thought* she was younger! Her mother tricked her!"

ABSINTHE ROSEMARY HIGHTOPP (tipping a hat made of shredded plea deals):

"She lied about her age more than once, when it suited her, when it paid off, when it shielded blame.
She wore deception like a debutante's perfume.
And baby, it lingered."

JUDGE FIDELLE WRATH (pounding gavel made of garden root):

"Enough. The math is not mathing.
Motion denied on the grounds of adult accountability."

"Let's stop pretending murder becomes excusable when you wrap it in sparkles and baby talk."

VONDA LYNNE HEARSPRAY

"But she wore glitter!"
"She didn't know any better!"

ABSINTHE ROSEMARY HIGHTOPP:

She was strategic, not innocent.

"That wasn't a breakdown; it was just a casting call."

"And that line?
'I'm too sick. I can't go to jail'?
That wasn't about diagnosis. That was about optics."

👨‍⚖️ GALLERY GASP – *Courtroom Reaction Theater*

- A juror's pen drops.
- A Endless Story Channel movie script gets torn in half.
- "Wait, she *knew*?"
- "*She used the Oracle?*"
- "That ain't no tutu tantrum."

JUDGE FIDELLA ETERNITY WRATH:

"Sustained in favor of the crows.
Let the record show:
She gambled you would mistake performance for panic.
But the Garden remembers."

She did not ask for help.
She asked for **leniency**.
She did not panic. She **performed**.
She did not confess. She **cast herself**.

"I'm too sick. I can't go to jail."
"Sir, I need a lawyer."
And she did not say it as a confused little minor child.
She said it as a grown woman who thought she could outmaneuver the truth.

✉️ *From the Clematis to the Violets*
"She said she was too sick. But we remember when she danced through our petals in secret, no wheels in sight."
– Garden of Silent Witnesses

🧠 Act 1, Scene 15: Bone Shard Glossary Entry 1

SECTION HEADER: Bone Shard Glossary
FILED BY: Fancy Macelli
FILED UNDER: Bone Shard Glossary Appendix
REALM: Forensic

🚩 Beat 1 ~ Narrative Pivot Delay

Filed Under: Psychological Defense Strategies – Crisis Narrative Management
A forensic term describing the intentional withholding or redirection of a story's emotional core until external reactions are gauged. Often used to reframe motive post hoc and build public sympathy.

🪶 Beat 2 ~ Example from Case:

Gypsy did not mention abuse until hours after initial questioning. Instead, she pivoted to illness and legal innocence. Trauma only entered the narrative after the mirror cracked.

🎯 Beat 3 ~ Direct from the Evidence Box

What was the first lie she told?
It was not about Dee Dee.
It was not about medical abuse.
It wasn't about fear.
It was this:

"I didn't know she was dead."
"I didn't help him."
"I was kidnapped."
"He raped me."

None of those things were true.
And none of them had anything to do with Munchausen, a wheelchair, or medicine.
The script did not start with sympathy.
It started with sabotage.
That is your first clue.

💜 Violet's Whisper

"It was not an outcry. It was a soft lie dressed in organza and pity."
She did not scream for help.
She whispered a line she knew would sell:

"I am too sick. I can't go to jail."
And when that did not land hard enough,
"Sir, I need a lawyer."

But not because she was scared.
Because she realized the audience was not clapping yet.

Act 1, Scene 16: The Mask, the Mirror, and the Misdirection

SECTION HEADER: 🪞 Mirror Tactics - Forensic Illusion vs. Confession
FILED BY: Fancy Macelli
FILED UNDER: Performance Psychology - Interrogation Theater - Strategic Myth making
REALM: Forensic

Gypsy's behavior in the first 48 hours was not a trauma confession. It was a performance rehearsal. What you are watching is not collapse, it is curation.

This forensic pattern is not rare.
We see it in **Erin Caffey**, who planned the slaughter of her entire family and told police she "just wanted to be with him."
We see it in **Jennifer Pan**, who ordered a hit on her parents and feigned shock as EMTs pulled her father's bleeding body out of the home.
And we see it in **Nicholas Godejohn**, who sat in his interrogation wearing innocence like an ill-fitting jacket, parroting Gypsy's lines until the truth started leaking.

In all these cases, there was a script.
And in all these cases, the first words out of their mouths were strategic, **not sincere**.

Gypsy did not confess because she was remorseful.
She confessed when she realized she had already been caught.
And even then, she tried to reframe it, not with facts, but with **emotion**.
"I'm too sick."
"I need a lawyer."
"I loved my momma."

But there was no love in the duct tape.
No grief in the texts.
No fear in the plan.
Just a glitter-dusted exit wound disguised as victimhood.

That is the danger of believing the **first version** of a story.
Especially when it is written for an audience.

Act 1, Scene 17: Garden Interlude – "The Echo That Didn't Cry"

SECTION HEADER: ≈ Transitional Reflection – Soundcheck for a Silenced Orchid
FILED BY: Miss Petunia Verity Cawington
FILED UNDER: Mourning Gaps – Posthumous Perspective – Witness Absence
REALM: Allegorical

The first 48 hours after the Mourning Orchid death did not echo with grief.
They echoed with manipulation.
With retellings. With strategic tears.
But there was no one crying for the Mourning Orchid.
No one placed flowers for the woman in the pink bedroom.
No one noticed the silence in the Garden.

 *Petunia's Postmark* (closing whisper):

"Before the girl learned to lie for the cameras, the mother had already died in silence."

Act 1, Scene 15: The First Lie Did Not Need a Scalpel, It Needed an Audience

SECTION HEADER: The Surgery That Lit the Fire
FILED BY: Amy Mackey & Fancy Macelli
FILED UNDER: Narrative Mistruths- Inciting Incidents
REALM: Forensic

Beat 1 ~ The Inciting Incident

In *My Time to Stand*, Gypsy identifies a throat surgery as the final straw. She tells readers her mother intended to **"cut [her] throat,"** not metaphorically, but medically, framing this ENT referral as imminent danger. She describes this moment as when she fully realized her mother's malice and plotted to have her murdered.

But the timeline contradicts her memory.

There was **no ENT referral, no pulmonology workup, and no scheduled surgery** in the summer or fall of 2015. Records show the **ENT consult describes what** happened in **2009**, tied to a now-defunct sleep apnea investigation that never progressed to surgery. What she presents as a surgical ambush was, in fact, a consultation that never became more than a note.

🜔 This is not a misremembered event, it is what psychologists call **emotional alibi construction**: dramatizing memory to justify future actions and reassign moral weight. She was not **describing** a crime. She was **reframing it** as defense.

This is where **symbolic distortion** enters the forensic frame.

Beat 2 ~ Documented Contradiction:

- Gypsy claims a decision for an imminent throat surgery in 2015.
- 📄 **No surgical referrals or hospital admission notes** appear in the records for that date range (See Medical Records, 2009–2015)
- She told Nick:
- "The only way for us to be together is for you to kill her."
- She layered it with-
- "I'm scared."
- "She's abusing me."
- "I need help."

Her words were **transactional intent layered in fantasy logic**.
Her fear, calculated.
Her directive was clear.

Dee Dee had to die. The end!

This was not a cry from a cornered child.
It was a script handed to the only person willing to act it out.

It marked the psychological handoff, **from plausible desperation to premeditated manipulation**.

Gypsy was not begging for rescue.
She was orchestrating the plot.
And that line?
It was not a secret.
It was a setup.

 *Nest Note:*

"She did not remember danger. She reframed regret."

Beat 3 ~ Symbolic Violence and Scar Logic

The most chilling part?
She admits it herself: *"You know, the neck is considered the most vulnerable part of the human body."*
Gypsy links her **emotional trauma** to the **physical scar** on her neck, describing prior surgeries as **"brutalizing,"** and her body as a battlefield. She directly references:
- **The scar from her salivary gland surgery**,
- Her **loss of voice**, and
- Her mother "muzzling" her.

And then she says it:
🔗 *"That scar that isn't there... that always travels with me."*

👉 That is not a reference to trauma prevention. That is regret for an act completed, **a psychic justification for murder**.
Her account implies that **Dee Dee's symbolic threat to her voice box** had to be repaid.
And when Gypsy chose the method of her mother's killing?
She did not pick poison.
She did not ask Nick to suffocate her.
She nearly decapitated her head.

This is what trauma therapists call **body mapping revenge**, an unconscious attempt to reassert control over one's violated body by replicating violence at the symbolic site of pain.

⚖️ Beat 4 ~ The First Truth She Decided to Tell

🎯 Prompt to the Jury:
What was the very first medical lie Gypsy Rose ever admitted to, not under cross-examination, not during interrogation, but in her own words?

It was not about feeding tubes.
It was not about wheelchairs.
It was not about being beaten, drugged, or starved.

It was this:

📱 *"I had a seizure at age six and after that, I could walk. But I never told anyone."*
➡️ *Text Message to Nick Godejohn*

And later:

📱 *"I have 1q21.1 microdeletion. That is why I had all those problems."*
➡️ *Text Message to Aleah*

📌 So ask yourself,
if she could walk and **chose not to tell**, who was she protecting?
If she knew her real diagnosis, **why didn't she mention it to investigators**?
If this was about fear... **why does the evidence point to strategy**?

💭 **Psychological Insight:**
These are not trauma-induced memory gaps.
They are *curated confessions*, timed and tailored for emotional manipulation.

This was not an outcry.
It was an **audition**.
And these messages were not slipped under a door begging for help,
they were placed like chess pieces, **knowing exactly what the audience would see**.

Beat 5 ~ Verdict Prompt:

"She did not confess to being abused.
She confessed to knowing the truth and hiding it."

Beat 6 ~ Forensic Cue:

This is the point where the **medical manipulation myth** collapses under its own weight. Not because Gypsy said so. But because **she said the opposite when she thought no one was looking.**

Her **first version** was not trauma-laced.

It was **performance polished**.

And this time, the audience did not ask for receipts but a lot of us brought them anyway.

Beat 7 ~ Bone Shard Glossary Entry 2: Emotional Alibi Construction

This behavior is consistent with a forensic pattern called **emotional alibi construction**, the post hoc dramatization of past events to rationalize later harm. It is not about memory distortion. It is about **memory weaponization.**

She was not recalling a trauma.
She was **framing a motive.**

 Definition

Emotional Alibi is a forensic psychology concept that refers to a narrative constructed by a defendant or suspect in which they retroactively embed emotional distress or trauma into the timeline of a crime to reduce perceived culpability. It works as a **narrative defense**, not a legal one crafted to elicit sympathy and reposition intent as reactive rather than premeditated.

According to Vecchi (2009), emotional alibis "allow offenders to distance themselves from the conscious agency behind their criminal decisions, typically by embedding a trauma-narrative or psychological trigger into the motivational backdrop of the crime."

Act 1, Scene 19: Is this Déjà vu?

SECTION HEADER: Where the World Intersects the Lie
FILED BY: Amy Mackey & Fancy Macelli
FILED UNDER: Forensic Evaluation- Murderous Narratives
REALM: Forensic

📖 Beat 1 ~ Application in the Gypsy Rose Blanchard Case

Gypsy's retrospective framing of the alleged 2015 "throat surgery" threat acts as an emotional alibi. Her *My Time to Stand* account turns a 2009 ENT consultation into an imminent, life-threatening act, retroactively inserting emotional stakes that did not exist at the time. This narrative distortion reframes premeditation as desperation, an intentional psychological maneuver often seen in mitigation storytelling.

🧪 Beat 2 ~ Case Study for Comparison: Diane Downs

1. Diane Downs

Emotional alibi was employed through her claims of escaping an abusive relationship and acting out of fear rather than intent. However, evidence showed clear premeditation and inconsistencies in her retelling of events like Gypsy's use of a distorted timeline and exaggeration of medical trauma. (Olsen, A. ,1987).

2. Jennifer Pan

Staged a home invasion where her mother was killed and father severely injured.
- Claimed years of strict "tiger parenting" drove her to desperation.
Emotional Alibi Used: Her narrative of emotional suffocation helped *some* media frame her as a tragic figure rather than a conspirator.

3. Casey Anthony

Told investigators her daughter was kidnapped by a nanny that did not exist.
- Eventually pivoted to a defense of alleged childhood abuse and emotional trauma to justify her erratic behavior and delayed reporting.
Emotional Alibi Used: Used victimhood to avoid direct accountability.

🎯 Beat 3 ~ Key Traits of Emotional Alibis:

- Often **post-hoc** justification
- Rooted in *emotion*, not *evidence*
- Employ metaphor, distortion, or partial truths
- Aim to redirect guilt or dilute motive
- Heavily used in media retellings to sway public sympathy

Gypsy's **emotional alibi** is not anchored in medical records, it is anchored in metaphor, memory distortion, and retrospective justification.
It reframes her role from **architect** to **actor**, from **planner** to **pawn**.

But emotional resonance is not the same as forensic truth.

And in a court of public opinion?
That difference changes everything.

Beat 4 ~ Direct Message Evidence: When the Script Breaks

Two private messages, one to **Aleah**, one to **Nick**, shatter any illusion of spontaneous confession or post-traumatic clarity.

🧬 To Aleah: The Gene That Disappeared When the Cameras Rolled

"They found the microdeletion, 1q21.1. That is what caused all the medical problems."

In this text, Gypsy directly links her medical conditions to a **genetic diagnosis**, a **chromosomal deletion that causes developmental delay, cognitive instability, and seizure susceptibility.** She acknowledges its **real existence** and its **long-term influence** on her health. Not fake. Not fabricated. Not imagined by her mother.

So why does this **never appear in her public defense**?

Because the **truth undermines the myth.**
If the medical issues had real, documentable roots, then **the Munchausen narrative collapses.**

🗨️ To Nick: The Seizure, the Secret, and the Chosen Lie

"When I was six, I had a seizure. After that I could walk again but I didn't tell anyone. I kept it a secret."

In our opinion, this is a confession of **intentional deception.**

Gypsy did not regain the ability to walk and get "forced" back into the chair.
She **hid** the truth.
She **chose** to play the role.
And she played it for **fifteen more years**.
Gypsy was **performing to remain loyal to a narrative that benefited her.**

📁 Beat 5 ~ Cumulative Impact:

These two messages reveal what no documentary, interview, or podcast has dared to say:

- Gypsy **knew she had a real medical condition.**
- Gypsy **knew she could walk.**
- Gypsy **chose not to tell anyone.**
- Gypsy **used fantasy logic and manipulated memory** to justify murder.
- And worst of all: she **said none of this in her interrogation or courtroom testimony.**

Why?

Because it doesn't sell.

🪶 Crow's Note:

"You can't retroactively erase the diagnosis or pretend the lie didn't have an opening night."

🎭 Act 1, Scene 16: Objection, Your Honor: She Had a Genetic Script!

SECTION HEADER: Where the World Intersects the Lie
FILED BY: Petunia Verity Cawington
FILED UNDER: Narrative Backfire - Sympathy Deflation - Prosecutorial Sass
REALM: Allegorical

[Interior – Courtroom. Lights up on Day Three of testimony.]

👨‍⚖️ **JUDGE FIDELLA ETERNITY WRATH:**
"Next witness, prosecution, proceed."

ABSINTHE ROSEMARY HIGHTOPP
"Ladies and gentlemen of the jury, today's exhibit is not from a hospital.
It is not from a chart.
It is not even from a Garden Archive dump.

It is from Gypmydia herself, via text.

'I have the Curse of the Crown. That is why I had all those problems.'

Simple sentence.
No duress.
No threats.
No spoon-fed story.

And to her boyfriend Prince Silas Gideon March:

"I'm just masquerading as a cripple for attention and of course free things. Even the Queen. She'll never see the betrayal coming."

So... tell me again...**who lied**?"

👩‍⚖️ **BRIETTA SLANDERELLA GASLIETTE VON OBJECTIONEE (clutching pearls):**
But Your Honor! Her *mother* made her say that!

ABSINTHE ROSEMARY HIGHTOPP
She *typed* it, sweetheart. No ventriloquism involved. Unless we are claiming the ghost of Cordelia, The Mourning Orchid, hijacked her Petal Phone.

👩‍⚖️ JUDGE FIDELLA ETERNITY WRATH:
Sustained. Prosecutor may continue. De LuLu, sit down. And stop waving that broken tiara.

ABSINTHE ROSEMARY HIGHTOPP
We are not arguing about interpretation.
We are arguing about *memory laundering*.
And guess what?
She did not just know the truth,
she *quoted it*.
Then buried it.

She weaponized her diagnosis as a shield when it served her and hid behind a fantasy when it did not."

🎯 *Final Strike:*

"She did not inherit a syndrome.
She inherited an audience.
And she played the part until the credits rolled,
then sued for syndication."

Garden Glossary Entry 1: The Curse of the Crown (allegorical term for Gypsy's chromosomal microdeletion)

A rare genetic fracture in the royal diadem of one's being an invisible crack in the crown that shapes the body's development and health. In the Garden's lore, it is the ancestral curse passed quietly through the bloodline, altering the bearer's path before they ever take their first step.

Though unseen by the casual observer, its influence can ripple through growth, cognition, and resilience, leaving the crown's jewels slightly askew.

Here, it is not a mark of shame but of origin, a truth written into the body's blueprint long before the weeds of falsehood took root.

In the world beyond the Garden's hedges, this curse is a medical fact: a documented chromosomal microdeletion with tangible effects, standing apart from the stories spun to mask or exploit it.

🧠 Act 1, Scene 21: Bone Shard Glossary Entry 3 & 4

SECTION HEADER: Bone Shard Glossary
FILED BY: Fancy Macelli & Amy Mackey
FILED UNDER: Trauma Rhetoric - Symbolic Violence - Narrative Psychology
REALM: Forensic

Beat 1 ~ Narrative Restitution & Body Mapping Revenge

Narrative Restitution (n.)
A psychological defense mechanism where a speaker "repays" perceived past harms by rewriting them into moral justification for later actions. This often includes exaggeration, metaphor-as-memory, or emotional alibis presented as unshakable truth.

Body Mapping Revenge (n.)
A trauma-driven behavioral pattern in which the site of physical violation becomes the site of retributive violence. Most common in cases of somatic trauma, long-term medical manipulation, or sexual abuse, this concept explains why some perpetrators reenact their pain on another's body in the same location.

🩸 *Example:* A woman with surgical trauma to her neck later chooses to stab her mother repeatedly in the throat, interpreted as an unconscious act of symbolic justice rather than targeted self-defense.

🖍 *Note:* Body mapping revenge does not equal healing. It is not catharsis. It is displacement. The violence is not directed inward but repackaged outward projected onto a symbolic scapegoat.

Act 1, Scene 22: Garden Gavel Moment

SECTION HEADER: Garden Interruptions & Allegorical Commentary
FILED BY: Tangie Lysithea Hara
FILED UNDER: Garden Gavel Moment- Selective Cherry Picking of Facts- Narrative Forensics - Pre-Rewrite Reconstruction
REALM: Allegorical

Beat 1 ~ The Diagnosis Stands

"Let the record show:
The Curse of the Crown was documented.
The diagnosis was delivered.
And the only thing fabricated... was the tale that followed.

You do not get to cherry-pick chromosomes, sugarcoat synapses, or redact reality because it does not fit your fairytale.

And in this Garden, we do not compost the truth just to fertilize a better headline.

This was not a case of false illness.
It was a case of inconvenient inheritance.
And when they could not bury the file...
They buried the meaning."

🖤 *The diagnosis stands.*
🖤 *The lies fall.*
🖤 *And the silence ends here.*

- T.L.H

 ### Beat 2 ~ Witness Bench Break ~ The Motel, the Wheelchair, and the Lie That Learned to Walk

PETUNIA VERITY CAWINGTON:
"When a girl walks out of a motel but ends up back in a chair three days later?
That is fiction written on hospital letterhead."

RUBY BEGONIA CAWINGTON:
"I saw the file. Cordelia didn't lie first.

The girl said, 'Don't tell anyone I can walk.'
That is not a cry for help. That's choreography."

WIDOW RUE:
"She didn't fake a sickness. She *wore* one."

PETUNIA VERITY CAWINGTON (softly):
"They didn't just bury The Mourning Orchid.
They buried the diagnosis too."

🌿 Act 1, Scene 23: "She Did Not Run from Danger. She Ran from the Narrative."

SECTION HEADER: The Weeds Speak What's Between the Cracks
FILED BY: The Weeds Compost Committee
FILED UNDER: Forgotten Fairytales- Truthful Skirting
REALM: Allegorical

Beat 1 ~ Beneath the Floorboards

We watched from beneath the floorboards of her fairytale,
buried in mulch and memory.
She did not flee into safety;
she fled into storytelling.
And when the petals started to fall,
she plucked them herself
and blamed the wind.

We saw how she rehearsed her lines.
How she softened the sharpest truths with powdered sugar.
And how the world leaned in,
not because they were fooled,
but because they liked the flavor better that way.

Truth does not vanish on its own.
It gets buried.
In sympathy.
In performance.
In perfect lighting and practiced tears.

She did not rewrite history, but she sure restaged it.

🌷 Beat 2 ~ Garden of Silent Witnesses

"The flowers heard it all   and they chose silence."

When Gypsy began spinning her myth of captivity and helplessness,
she was not doing it in a vacuum.

There were witnesses.
There were friends.

There were family members.
There were doctors, nurses, neighbors, classmates, and charity organizers,
all of whom saw the cracks in the image she portrayed.

They saw her walk when she thought no one was looking.
They heard her laugh in parking lots, free and vibrant.
They watched her flirt, shop, cosplay, scheme.
They read the text messages that did not match the trembling voice she used on stage.

And yet,
they said nothing.
Or worse, they excused it.

In Wonderland, silence is not innocence.
It's complicity.
The garden was not fooled.
It was simply too enchanted to resist the lie.

 *Tiger-Lily's Note:*
"Even a flower with thorns can pretend not to notice the blood it blooms in."

Act 1, Scene 24: Damsel, Not Distressed

SECTION HEADER: Performance for Sympathy
FILED BY: Fancy Macelli & Amy Mackey
FILED UNDER: Playwright Prisoner- Damsel Not Distressed- False Hero Complex
REALM: Forensic

"They didn't find a prisoner. They found a playwright."

"It's a poor sort of memory that only works backward." - The White Queen

When the world met Gypsy Rose Blanchard,
they did not see a criminal.
They saw a captive.
A girl in a wheelchair.
A frail whisper of a voice.
A trembling hand clutching stuffed animals and survival stories.

But that was not the truth.
The "damsel" narrative did not begin with evidence.
It began with **performance**.

She was not imprisoned. She was auditioning.
And the media? The courts? The public?
They did not just accept it, but they also needed it.

Act 1, Scene 25: Petals That Bleed

SECTION HEADER: Abandoned Memory
FILED BY: Fancy Macelli & Amy Mackey
FILED UNDER: Disgraced in Death- The Jealous Sibling Factor
REALM: Forensic

Beat 1 ~ The Most Beautiful Gardens Often Hide the Deepest Wounds.

When Gypsy spun her story of survival, the world wept.
But no one wept for Dee Dee.
Not when she was alive.
Not when she was brutally murdered.

Because when sympathy gardens are tended,
only the flowers that fit the story are allowed to bloom.

Dee Dee's family abandoned her memory long before the grave.
Ten years in a box.
No urn.
No marker.
Just silence.

And even now, that urn sits empty.

Because grieving Dee Dee would mean confronting the lie.
And that is a garden no one wants to walk through.

 ## Violet Mourns:

"They painted over her thorns with red and called it healing. But even the petals knew what they were hiding."

Beat 2 ~ Closing Verdict Prompt:

She did not confess to being abused.
She confessed to *knowing the truth* and hiding it.
She did not flee from danger.
She fled into *narrative*.

And when that narrative broke...
She did not cry.

The world did.

Act 1, Scene 24: Exhibit B - Stranger in the Script

SECTION HEADER: Abandoned Memory
FILED BY: Fancy Macelli & Amy Mackey
FILED UNDER: Disgraced in Death- The Jealous Sibling Factor
REALM: Forensic

Beat 1 ~ When the Mother Becomes a Motive

From the opening line of *My Time to Stand*, Gypsy does not introduce Dee Dee as her mother. She introduces her as the woman who "gave life" to her, then immediately juxtaposes that with taking it away. It is surgical, poetic even, but cold. This is not a daughter recalling trauma. This is a narrator setting the stage for a necessary death.

She does not say, "My mom and I had a complicated relationship."
She says, *"At 24 years old Dee Dee Blanchard gave life to me... and at 23, one month from turning 24, I took life from her."*

There is no warmth. No anguish. No real sense of grief.

 **Mack put it best:** *"Gypsy refers to Dee Dee like she's a stranger."*

It is not just stylistic detachment. It is a legal strategy disguised as memoir. Because the further she can place Dee Dee from herself emotionally, the easier it is to paint the murder as righteous. If Dee Dee is a stranger, she is not a mother. She is a threat. A villain. A plot device.

This is not a memory. It is character blocking. And the script only works if the audience forgets there was once love in the room.

🖋 Crow's Note:

"She didn't grieve her mother; she rebranded her as the antagonist."

Act 1, Scene 27: The Campaign Started Right There

SECTION HEADER: Gypsy Rose Lied About It All
FILED BY: Fancy Macelli & Amy Mackey
FILED UNDER: Origin of the Narrative, Branding Over Truth
REALM: Forensic

It did not begin with Munchausen.
It did not begin with a feeding tube, a wheelchair, or a forged birth certificate.

The campaign began with a pivot.
And an audience.

When Gypsy folded in that interrogation room, not into grief, but into character, two people did not flinch. They leaned in.

Mike the attorney who never investigated the truth,
Kristy the stepmother, already booking interviews.

They did not build a defense.
They built a product.
And they sold her fast.

 *Crow's Note*

"She was not buried by a diagnosis.
She was reborn by a marketing team."

Act 1, Scene 28: Forensic Focus: The Diagnosis That Would Not Comply

SECTION HEADER: The Truth Behind All the Illnesses
FILED BY: Fancy Macelli & Amy Mackey
FILED UNDER: Undeniable Evidence- Narrative Omission Strategy
REALM: Forensic

The most dangerous lie Gypsy Rose Blanchard ever told wasn't that she was sick. It was pretending she never had been.

In her very first police interview following Dee Dee's murder, Gypsy did not cry about being abused. She did not mention wheelchairs or medications or feeding tubes. She did not even claim her mother had hurt her.

She said she had no idea her mother was dead.
She asked if Dee Dee had **killed herself**.
She told Detective Stan Hancock that her boyfriend and her mother did not get along, and that he must have lost control.
She claimed she had been **kidnapped**.
She said she had been **raped** by Nick.
She positioned herself as a frightened girl, held against her will, too afraid to intervene.

And **never once** did she mention Munchausen by proxy.

There was no talk of forced sedation.
No mention of abuse.
No claim of being held captive.
No suggestion that Dee Dee had fabricated her illnesses.

All of that came later.

Act 1, Scene 29: Bone Shard Glossary Entry: Narrative Pivot Delay

SECTION HEADER: Narrative Pivot Delay
FILED BY: Fancy Macelli & Amy Mackey
FILED UNDER: Timeline Twisters
REALM: Forensic

In forensic psychology, a *narrative pivot delay* occurs when a subject withholds or alters the core justification for an act until they gauge the consequences or public reaction. This is trial strategy.

📁 Beat 1 ~ Documented Timeline:

- June 15, 2015 - Initial Interrogation (Springfield Police Dept.)
  📄 Gypsy's Statements

- "I would never hurt my mom. I loved my momma. My mom was my best friend."
- "My mom and my boyfriend didn't get along."
- "He raped me."
- "I tried to stop him."
- "Maybe he can get the help he needs now. He is very disturbed."
- "I wasn't involved."
- "I didn't know she was dead."
- "I never should have left her."
- "Aleah's always been a bully to me."
- "Sir, I'm very sick, I can't go to jail."

The most famous line of all: "Sir, I need a lawyer." Proving she knew she could have one but did not think she would need one. She expected everyone to buy her lies hook, line, and sinker. Because why wouldn't they? They had always done so before. The thing is it almost worked if had not been for the internet and her annoying cell phone.

What's missing?
Everything that made her famous.

There is **no mention of abuse** until later.
There is **no mention of MBP** until Krusty Blanchard and Mike Stanfield reframe the story for press consumption.
There is **no claim of fabricated illnesses** until the HBO cameras start rolling.

The original script did not include a medical mystery.
It included a scapegoat.
And she handed it to the man she had spent years grooming.

Beat 2 ~ The Diagnosis That Refused to Disappear

However, buried in sealed records, FOIA documents, and genetic reports are a truth that unravels that entire myth. Gypsy was born with **1q21.1 microdeletion syndrome**, a rare chromosomal abnormality associated with mild to moderate intellectual disability, cognitive delays, and executive functioning challenges.

It is a legitimate genetic condition, one that cannot be faked, induced, or caused by environmental manipulation. It is diagnosed through genetic testing, not observation, not hearsay. The discovery of this microdeletion found in her files in 2011, blows the idea of medical child abuse out of the water.

Dr. Le Pichon at the Kansas City Children's Hospital, through extensive genetic testing on Gypsy and Dee Dee, identified the disorder and was able to confirm that Dee Dee was not the carrier and Rod was unavailable for testing, but that Gypsy had a mild to moderate deletion in Chromosome 1.

Between 2001 and 2015, Gypsy's medical file reflects a consistent clinical profile. Neuropsychological assessments documented **global developmental delays, fine motor coordination issues**, & **working memory impairment.** She showed deficits in abstract reasoning, processing speed, and adaptive behavior. These results aligned with known characteristics of the 1q21.1 deletion, which can affect both neurological development and behavior regulation.

And yet, in her memoir and media appearances, Gypsy refers to these verifiable facts only when absolutely necessary and often with disclaimers like, *"This is what I remember"* or *"This is how it felt to me."* More often, she leaves them out entirely. This is not an oversight. It is a pattern of narrative omission.

She wanted the world to believe that every diagnosis was a fabrication.
That every doctor had been fooled.
That her limitations were just the side effects of Dee Dee's imagination.

But before there were headlines, hashtags, or Hulu scripts,
there was the gene.
1q21.1 microdeletion syndrome: a rare, verifiable chromosomal disorder with documented effects on physical development, cognitive function, and executive processing.

It is not theatrical.
It is not exaggerated.
But it is real.

🧬 Beat 3 ~ Bone Shard Glossary Entry: Narrative Omission Strategy

In forensic psychology, this tactic is sometimes classified as a **Narrative Omission Strategy:** The deliberate exclusion of factual context that complicates or threatens the emotional clarity of a personal story. For Gypsy, acknowledging her diagnosis would mean confronting an uncomfortable reality: that Dee Dee may not have invented her illness, but instead was navigating a rare and poorly understood genetic disorder that required lifelong care.

When a subject deliberately excludes or minimizes facts that complicate a clean victim story, that's not trauma. That is editing.

And Gypsy edited out her diagnosis almost entirely.
Because nuance does not sell. Sympathy does.

📂 Beat 4 ~ Documented Truth: Medical Confirmation

Between 21 and 2015, the available medical and educational documentation shows:

- Diagnosed 1q21.1 microdeletion (a confirmed chromosomal deletion)
- Developmental delays seen across multiple specialties
- Homeschooling recommended due to cognitive and adaptive challenges
- Noted deficits in fine motor skills, speech, and processing speed
- Repeated evaluations pointing to learning difficulties and delayed executive function

These are not symptoms that can be staged.
They were witnessed, recorded, and assessed across multiple visits, many of which included hospital staff who had no personal allegiance to Dee Dee Blanchard and no incentive to falsify outcomes.

And yet in *My Time to Stand*, Gypsy offers none of it.

Beat 5 ~ Bone Shard Glossary Entry

📌 **Disassociation Strategy**
Definition: A psychological or rhetorical tactic in which a person distances themselves from parts of their identity, behavior, or history that threaten the credibility of their current narrative.

In Gypsy's case?
She does not argue the diagnosis was wrong.
She acts like it never mattered.
She uses it only when it helps evoke pity, then shelves it when it threatens her agency.

But you cannot erase a chromosome.
And you cannot overwrite a diagnosis just because it does not fit the new brand.

That reality doesn't sell. It does not generate headlines or movie deals. So, it was erased, not from the records, but from the retelling.

Gypsy did not deny the 1q21.1 diagnosis outright. She did something more insidious: she reframed it as part of Dee Dee's fantasy. She cast her actual cognitive and developmental symptoms as the results of poisoning or over-medication, never showing that they were documented years before any feeding tube, wheelchair, or pain medication entered the picture. She used this framework to suggest that her mental fog was a product of abuse, not biology. In doing so, she cut the most significant contradiction to her entire narrative: **that she was genuinely, medically different from other children her age.**

This disassociation from diagnosis served her in many ways. It allowed her to present herself as fully capable and sane while simultaneously pleading that she had been too cognitively impaired to know better. It is a sleight of hand, claiming clarity when it suits her and confusion when it does not. And because so few people are familiar with the implications of microdeletions like 1q21.1, the lie slid by unchallenged.

But the truth never left the file. And if you read closely, it is all there: the test results, the genetic report, the notes from multiple independent clinicians who described a young woman struggling with memory, planning, learning, and emotional regulation. Not because her mother made her but because that is what the chromosome said.

This was never a hoax.
It was a condition.
One she resented.
One she buried.
One that still sits, unmentioned, in the shadow of the myth she built in its place.

 Nest Note

"She did not break free from a false identity.
She deleted the one that didn't sell."

Act 1, Scene 30: Forensic Focus: The Lie That Did Not Live in the Room

SECTION HEADER: Narrative Shifts, Myth Invention, Tactical Rebranding
FILED BY: Fancy Macelli & Amy Mackey
FILED UNDER: Innocent Act- Kidnapping Narrative
REALM: Forensic

Beat 1 ~ The Innocent Fabrication

When Gypsy was first questioned by Springfield detectives in June 2015, she did not mention abuse.
She did not mention poison.
She did not claim she was sick, or that her mother made her sick.

She played innocent.

In fact, her original story had nothing to do with Munchausen by proxy. It was not about medical torture. It was a *kidnapping narrative*, constructed on the spot to explain why she was found in Wisconsin, alive and unharmed, while her mother's corpse was rotting in a pink bungalow in Missouri.

Her first version of events to Detective Hancock was this:

- Nick Godejohn had come to her house.
- He and her mother did not get along.
- He killed Dee Dee while she hid in the bathroom.
- She didn't know he planned it.
- She was afraid of him and went with him because she did not know what else to do.
- She even asked if her mother had committed suicide.
- Then she claimed Nick raped her.

Not one word of this was true.

She knew her mother was dead.
She gave Nick the pre-cut duct tape and a knife.
She knew because she asked him to.

And she left with him willingly, on camera.

The story unraveled the moment the detectives left the room. When she was alone, crouched by the door, listening through the crack, the performance shifted. She did not ask for her mother. She did not ask for protection. She said, *"I'm very sick. I can't go to jail."*

This is what forensic psychologists call *Emotional Alibi Construction*:
The use of emotional cues, real or staged, to shield the speaker from accountability.
It is not confession. It is a cover.

🧠 Beat 2 ~ Anatomy of a Lie

She did not ask for a lawyer because she was traumatized.
She asked because she knew that is what guilty people do when they are trying to get sympathy instead of sentencing.

Forensic Insight:
This is not a girl discovering fear.
It is a girl preloading her emotional defense before the facts are ever entered into evidence.

And it worked. Because within hours, the framework changed completely.

She had confessed, yes, but now she wasn't a killer.
She was a *sick girl*, trapped in an *abusive fantasy*, *forced* into the crime.

And that transformation did not come from Gypsy alone.

> It came from **Kristy**.
> From **Mike**.
> And from the early producers of what would become **HBO's, Mommy and Dearest Dead (Erin Lee Carr), and Hulu's, The Act (Michelle Dean).**

MBP was not the initial claim.
It was the retrofit.

They did not find a diagnosis in the file and ran with it.
They *needed* a diagnosis to explain the crime and **Munchausen by proxy** gave them a media-friendly label that absolved Gypsy and villainized Dee Dee in a single stroke.

But here is the forensic problem:

- MBP is extremely rare.
- It is never diagnosed posthumously.
- And it cannot be determined from hearsay.

Gypsy's real medical diagnosis, **1q21.1 deletion syndrome**, was ignored entirely.
Because it did not serve the new script. Her actual condition undermined the media-ready fable: that she had been *perfectly healthy*, *trapped*, and *falsely medicalized*.

So, they buried the real diagnosis.
And they sold the lie.

 **Nest Note:**

"She did not expose a lie, she replaced one."

🎭 Act 1, Scene 31: Why It Was Erased from the Script

SECTION HEADER: Narrative Erasure
FILED BY: Fancy Macelli & Amy Mackey
FILED UNDER: Script Doctoring- Facts Erased- Narrative Suppression- Diagnostic Distortion- Media Engineering
REALM: Forensic

🩺 Beat 1 ~ Script Doctoring: When the Truth Did not Fit the Role

Medical records do not make good monologues. So, they were buried beneath the better lines.

Some people look at Gypsy's ability to plan and perform and ask, *"Was she ever really impaired?"*

But that is the wrong question.

The issue is not whether she could function, it is **how** she adapted. In a world designed to constantly underestimate her, Gypsy did not just survive her limitations. She learned to camouflage them. It was not capability that defined her behavior.

It was **calculation**, sharpened by years of being perceived as helpless. What appeared was not strength, it was strategy. A kind of psychological choreography learned through reward, repetition, and performance.

A **learned helplessness** of sorts, only she didn't stay trapped in it. She learned how to use it.

Act 1, Scene 32: Bone Shard Glossary Entry 7: When Conditioning Becomes a Weapon

SECTION HEADER: Bone Shard Glossary
FILED BY: Fancy Macelli & Amy Mackey
FILED UNDER: Psychological Manipulation | Cognitive Adaptation | Identity Engineering
REALM: Forensic

 Beat 1 ~ Term: Learned Helplessness

Definition:
A psychological state in which a person, after repeated exposure to stress or failure, stops trying to change their circumstances, even when opportunities for escape or control exist.

In This Case:

But in Gypsy's case, it went one step further.

She did not just internalize helplessness.
She **studied** how the world responded to it.
She learned that frailty earned favors.
That silence evoked sympathy.
That people expect nothing from someone who appears broken.

And then she used it.

Her behavior shows signs of what forensic psychologists call **manipulative passive dependency**, a pattern where helplessness is not a condition, but a tool.
A survival mechanism that becomes performance art.

 Beat 2 ~ Clinical Insight:
- Learned helplessness often results from repeated traumatic or high-stakes environments.
- When reinforced by social or emotional reward (e.g., charity, praise, protection), it can transform into behavioral conditioning.
- In rare cases, individuals develop **strategic helplessness**, exaggerating or simulating dysfunction to reduce accountability. This is what Gypsy is doing.

Crow's Note:

"She didn't escape the cage." She learned how to decorate it and make you unlock the door."

The microdeletion wasn't convenient.
It muddled the myth.
It did not support her claim of being completely healthy and held hostage by fabricated disease.
It raised too many questions.

Because if she was cognitively delayed…
If she **did** have developmental limitations…
Then the story changes.
Then Dee Dee was not inventing illnesses
She was navigating real ones.
Then Gypsy was not just manipulated
She was a participant, limited but not lacking agency.

The moment you reintroduce the diagnosis, the motive starts to fracture.
And for Gypsy, that meant danger.

So, it vanished.
From interviews.
From documentaries.
And even in her book, it is brushed aside in a footnote like a rumor.

From Hulu specials to livestream Q&As, Gypsy has spent years minimizing, dodging, or outright denying the one thing that does not serve her victim arc: the microdeletion. Even in her memoir *My Time to Stand*, the genetic diagnosis is brushed aside in a single sentence, buried like a technicality.

It is never discussed with any medical detail, never contextualized, and never treated as meaningful. And while that sliver of acknowledgment exists in the print edition, it is *completely erased* from the audiobook version. Not abridged but removed. As if it never happened.

On her post-release press tour, she leaned in harder, telling followers she was "completely healthy" and that her mother was "never tested." She deflected questions about the disorder's impact and pivoted blame away from her father insisting *he* must not have it; therefore, he is not flawed or accountable either. Festering her own delusional denial.

There is no documentation of Rod being tested, and yet Gypsy & Kristy insist on this speculative exoneration, despite the known presence of neurological, psychiatric, and cognitive conditions within her paternal bloodline. The reality is that Dee Dee *was* ruled out as a carrier in 2011. And while it could theoretically be an isolated breakthrough, I challenge you to look at the pictures posted all over social media last year. It's one of Gypsy's first holiday pictures post prison release. Gypsy's paternal great grandmother is a dead ringer for Gypsy. Showing the physical anomalies.

And Gypsy's sudden attempt to shift the genetic shadow onto her dad and, by extension, Krusty Blanchard, her media-manager-stepmother-cousin is not just deflection. It's erasure. Of evidence. Of origin. Of accountability.

 *Nest Note:*

"She did not hide the file.
She just made sure no one read it."

Act 1, Scene 33: Genetic Ghost - The Diagnosis That Disappeared

SECTION HEADER: Forensic Sidebar
FILED BY: Fancy Macelli & Amy Mackey
FILED UNDER: Medical Erasure - Strategic Omission - Symbolic Distortion
REALM: Forensic

What happens when the most inconvenient piece of medical evidence does not support the narrative?
It vanishes.

The 1q21.1 microdeletion diagnosis, confirmed in 2011 by a licensed geneticist and ruled out in Dee Dee Blanchard, was once treated as the "answer" that explained Gypsy's lifelong symptoms. But today, it is a shadow cast out of every media frame Gypsy can control.

In her post-release media blitz, Gypsy declared on podcasts like *Barely Famous* and *MisSPELLING* that she is "completely healthy." She then claimed she is one of the "75% of people with 1q21.1 microdeletion who are unaffected" a statistic she has invented. That number is not cited in any scientific literature, and it directly contradicts the long-standing medical research, which shows the disorder can cause a range of significant cognitive and neurological impacts, even when physically subtle.

Even more alarming is how *My Time to Stand* treats the diagnosis.
In the print edition? One sentence.
In the audiobook? Not included at all.

It was not abridged.
It was redacted.

Meanwhile, Kristy, the stepmother, cousin, and self-appointed media manager, has tried to label the microdeletion as "borderline," a term that does not apply in genetic classification. There is no such thing as a *partial* microdeletion. Even the smallest deletions can cause profound disruptions. Kristy's choice of phrasing downplays what geneticists recognize as a valid, explanatory syndrome simply because it weakens the abuse mythology, she helped market.

And to explain away the diagnosis, Gypsy now blames Dee Dee. She claims her mother never got tested (false) and that her father did but has shown no proof of such testing for Rod or her child Aurora. Cognitive or neurological challenges documented in his family history only further complicate that claim.

The deletion did not disappear.
It was scrubbed for strategic reasons.
Because if Gypsy *was* cognitively delayed
Then Dee Dee was not inventing illnesses.
She was managing one.
And that fractures everything.

📁 Act 1, Scene 34: The Terms That Convict: Medical Child Abuse by Any Other Name

SECTION HEADER: Forensic Sidebar
FILED BY: Fancy Macelli & Amy Mackey
FILED UNDER: Diagnostic Distortion- Prosecutorial Insight- Narrative Engineering
REALM: Forensic

🔖 Beat 1 ~ Expert Commentary: Mike Weber, Medical Child Abuse Specialist, Tarrant County DA's Office

"What's the difference between a con family choosing this as their hustle and a Munchausen mom?"
"Nothing."
– Mike Weber, MCA Investigative Expert

It would be a great joke, but we are missing the punch line. I had a phone conversation with Mike in spring of 2024. This was where I posed the question above and got the simple answer. "Nothing." No more explanation needed.

Gypsy Rose never once says "medical child abuse." Not in her book. Not in her interviews. Not in her viral rebranding tour. The phrase *Munchausen by proxy* does not even appear until after her legal team and media fixers took the wheel. But according to seasoned investigators like Mike Weber, that is no oversight, but it is certainly narrative control.

Weber, whose record of convictions in MCA cases sets a national standard, does speak plainly about what works, and what fails, in court.

"We don't lead with Munchausen by proxy. We call it what it is: child abuse. And when you say *child abuse*, juries understand. The intent, the diagnosis, the motive, none of that changes the outcome. It's still a child being harmed under the guise of care."

In his experience, the complexity of MBP or FDIA too often becomes a smokescreen. So, he simplifies not the abuse, but the language.

Because language convicts. And in this case, it also protects.

By the time *Mommy Dead and Dearest* aired, the phrase "Munchausen by proxy" had become its tagline. The words rolled off every anchor's tongue. It was the shorthand the media needed, the buzzword the audience clung to.

But in the actual courtroom?

- No psychiatric expert was ever called to testify.
- No formal diagnosis was made.
- No mental health evaluation of Dee Dee was presented by the defense or the prosecution.

The phrase was not a clinical conclusion.
It was a posthumous weapon.
A narrative insertion.
Not a medical fact.

So, what was erased?

The truth.

Medical child abuse, unlike Munchausen by proxy confusing term, does not require a motive. It does not require a psychological label. It does not even require that the parent be mentally ill.

What it does require... is harm.

And Gypsy never told *that* version.
Because that version required accountability.

And as for the family?

Not even one of Dee Dee's siblings, those who now mourn her publicly on Facebook or request sympathy in interviews, spoke up in her defense when it mattered most. Not when the tabloids ran wild. Not when Gypsy called her a monster. Not when Hulu immortalized the lie.

They stayed silent.

They had the chance to say: "This isn't true."
They did not.

Instead, they let the myth breathe because they, too, benefited from the publicity. The same family who now claims to feel "devastated" never once contested Gypsy's claims on record. Not in court. Not in press. Not in protest.

And what is worse?

We now know how Clauddinea Pitre felt.
Because her letters, her voicemails, and her medical history speak louder than any headline.
She was not perfect.
But she was present.

She fought to raise her daughter despite unrelenting challenges, systemic failures, and profound isolation.

And in return, not one person stood for her.
Not in life.
And certainly not in death.

Now, a decade later, they ask for sympathy.
But they still will not dispute the lie.

We do not see this as them expressing grief, we see them being complicit.

Act 1, Scene 33: The Four Masks of Medical Deception

SECTION HEADER: A Rose by Any Other Name
FILED BY: Fancy Macelli & Amy Mackey
FILED UNDER: Diagnostic Disambiguation | Forensic Psychology | Intent vs. Performance
REALM: Forensic

Not all deceptions wear the same face. And not every lie fits snugly inside a DSM box. So, let us clarify the clinical and legal distinctions between the terms that keep getting misused, confused, or deliberately entangled when talking about Gypsy Rose and Dee Dee Blanchard:

🧠 Beat 1 ~ Munchausen Syndrome (aka Factitious Disorder on Self)

A person feigns, exaggerates, or induces illness in *themselves* to gain attention, care, or emotional reward.
  📌 *Example*: A person fakes seizures to be admitted to the hospital and receive sympathy.

🧠 Beat 2 ~ Munchausen by Proxy (MBP) (aka FDIA)

A caregiver, often a parent, induces or fabricates illness in *another* (usually a child), for similar attention-seeking motives.
  📜 *What's key*: The perpetrator is motivated not by financial gain, but by emotional validation.
  💊 *Legal complication*: Often misused in court because FDIA requires proving psychiatric intent.

💰 Beat 3 ~ Malingering

The feigning of illness *for material gain*, money, drugs, freedom, benefits. This is *not* a mental illness. It is a behavior pattern rooted in manipulation.
  📌 *Example*: Pretending to be disabled to secure disability benefits or avoid prosecution.

💰 Beat 4 ~ Malingering by Proxy

A rarely discussed but critical term, used when a caregiver fabricates or exaggerates illness in someone else *for material gain* rather than emotional gratification.
✦ *Translation:* It is not about "being seen." It is about what being seen *gets you*.

Beat 5 ~ Field Notes from the Prosecutor's Desk

Medical Child Abuse (MCA):

The above terms can confuse a jury faster than a politician can break a promise. By terming this as medical child abuse it puts it in clear terms.

Definition: A caregiver deliberately exaggerates, fabricates, or induces medical symptoms in a child, leading to unnecessary medical interventions and direct harm.

- **Key Element:** The abuse is behavioral, not psychological. A psychiatric diagnosis of the caregiver is not needed.
- **Legal Focus:** The child's experience not the parent's presumed illness or backstory, drives the case.
- **Courtroom Implication:** When framed as MCA, the case centers on harm. When framed as MBP, it centers on the caregiver's *why*, and opens the door for confusion, sympathy, and ambiguity.

🪶 Crow's Note:

"They did not need a label. They needed a legal hook. So, they picked the one that sold best and left the truth behind."

🪶 Beat 6 ~ Crowsplain It to Me

So where does Gypsy fall? And where does Dee Dee?

Let's be fair.
Dee Dee Blanchard may very well have used aspects of Gypsy's conditions to their advantage.
But what single mother, with serious health problems of her own, a manipulative child actively lying about her own abilities, and a deadbeat dad she chased for medical bills and support was supposed to do?

Yes, Dee Dee leaned into the narrative.
Yes, she accepted the charity and played the part.
But she was not inventing diagnoses.
She was not forcing symptoms that did not exist.
She was not creating a sick child. She was managing one.
And often, she was doing it alone.

This was not Munchausen by proxy.
It was not some elaborate long con orchestrated by a fame-hungry matriarch.
It was survival. Messy, morally murky, often desperate survival.

But Gypsy?
She knew exactly what she was doing.

She admitted to Aleah that she had the microdeletion.
She told Nick she had been able to walk since she was six.
She continued the ruse for over a decade, not out of fear, but out of function.
Because the con worked.
It got her attention.
It got her gifts.
It got her power.

"I had a procedure at 6 and I had a seizure and was temporarily paralyzed. They didn't know if I'd get feeling back or not. Eventually I started to, but I never told my mom or doctors because I was scared mom would stop loving me."
- Gypsy Rose Blanchard, text message to Nicholas Godejohn in 212

This was not about protection. We see this as more performance.

She did not support the lie to survive her mother.
She maintained it to manipulate everyone else.

Because if she could walk,
she could leave.
She could report.
She could escape.

That is why the "abuse arc" begins to collapse here. Because Gypsy was not just trapped in a lie. She was co-writing it.

And the moment she admitted otherwise, the entire house of cards came down.

So, no, Gypsy was not a prisoner.
She was a co-author.
And the narrative was not imposed on her.
It was a script she rehearsed long before the cameras arrived.

Beat 7 ~ Receipts from the Record

- FOIA medical reports note malingering behavior flagged by physical therapists in Missouri as early as 2009 - Multiple witnesses saw Gypsy walking without aid in Aurora, Missouri, years before the murder.
- She admitted to Nick Godejohn that she could walk "since age 6."
- She was caught in 2009 during an attempted runaway, *in a hotel room, walking freely.*

Beat 8 ~ Wonderland Echo: The Chair Was a Choice

The real ruse was not Dee Dee's alone.
Gypsy was not just cast in the play.
She stayed for the encore.

🩸 Act 1, Scene 35: The Ruse Was Already Up ~ Scene, Rewrite, Performance

SECTION HEADER: The Ruse Timeline
FILED BY: Fancy Macelli & Amy Mackey
FILED UNDER: Lies & Contradictions- Medical Malfeasance
REALM: Forensic

Beat 1 ~ Medical Malfeasance

She says it in *My Time to Stand* like it is a climactic reveal:

"The ruse was up."

But what *ruse*, exactly?

Because by 2009, **six years before the murder**, Gypsy was already walking. Already sneaking away. Already disappearing into motel rooms with grown men.
She was not a sick child held hostage.
She was a cognitively delayed teenager balancing fantasy, fetish, and fraud.

📒 **Confirmed Witnesses**:
- Neighbors in Aurora, Missouri recall seeing her walk unaided.
- Hospital staff from her 2009 runaway incident noted no assistive equipment.
- At least one Springfield resident saw Gypsy upright, mobile, and engaged in conversation years before June 2015.

So, if "the ruse was up," it was not because Dee Dee got caught.
It was because Gypsy **knew Dee Dee knew**.

And when your entire performance depends on a lie being airtight, there is only one direction left to go when that seal breaks:
Destruction.
Not escape.
Not justice.
Erasure.

This was not about the diagnosis. It was not even about the abuse.
It was about control, **narrative control**.

📅 Beat 2 ~ Timeline Insert: Spring 2011 - The Fuse Is Lit

Let's examine the **four-month tailspin** that rewired Gypsy's trajectory:

- **February 2011** – She begins corresponding with "Dan," a 36-year-old parolee. Gypsy was 19 but told Dan she was 15.
  Dan claims she was sexually aggressive and obsessive, later telling others he had to block her.
  Gypsy would later call him a pedophile in a text to Aleah…after he rejected her. The obsessive attachment? Still ongoing in 223, per intercepted texts and letters.
- **March 2, 2011** – Gypsy is diagnosed with **1q21.1 microdeletion**.
  Dee Dee is ruled out as the carrier.
  This diagnosis not only explains many of Gypsy's symptoms but also directly challenges the myth of total fabrication.
  The diagnosis should have ended the charade. Instead, it triggered a new one.
- **May 17–21, 2011** – She sends **nude photos** to her father **Rod**, and her 10-year-old half-sister **Mia**, asking Mia to help her find Dan on Facebook.
  She posts a Facebook rant calling Rod a "deadbeat" who "ruined her life."
Rod had another daughter, Nicolette, also estranged.
At the time of Gypsy's post, she did not even know Nicolette existed.

- **June 2011** – She shoots Dee Dee with a **BB gun**, ten times.
  No media picked it up. No child protection was called.
  But the message was clear. Dee Dee was a liability and becoming increasingly more problematic as her health declined. Dee Dee had to go, and brutal murder was the choice Gypsy made.

⚖️ Beat 3 ~ The Contradiction Amplified:

Kristy Blanchard now openly admits that the family knew Gypsy had a preference for older men—men in their 30s and 40s—and, in her words, "they supported it because she was 18."

Some sources from the VisionCon group have stated that Gypsy and Dee Dee were in a Facebook group for the convention fans and that Gypsy openly flirted with older men. Indicating Dee Dee was not as in control as Gypsy would have the public believe. This is supported by Gypsy's online posting of her role-playing Anna Steele, from *"Fifty Shades of Grey."* She later told Nick that was the first movie she wanted to watch with him right after the boxed set of *"True Blood"* and *"Game of Thrones"* she packed for her trip to WI.

But here's the problem: Rod Blanchard's own oft-repeated "18th birthday" anecdote flatly contradicts that stance. In his version, Dee Dee told him that Gypsy believed she was only 14 years old at the time. If that's true, then any "support" for her pursuing sexual relationships with significantly older, and sometimes married, men would have been, by their own framing, support for a mentally delayed adult/child engaging with adult predators.

The contradiction gets worse with the evidence now in the record. FOIA-released materials and email archives show that Gypsy was engaging with older men online.

But to hear Kristy tell it, there was no cause for concern when Gypsy actively enlisted her 10-year-old sister to message at least one of them, Dan Glidewell, on her behalf.

These weren't teenage crushes. These were sexualized, adult conversations, sometimes with men deep into criminal activity. We also see from the email chains that Gypsy knew exactly how to maintain and juggle these interactions, even while hiding behind different senders and accounts.

So which version of reality is the Blanchard family asking the public to believe?
-The "forever 14" version, which paints Gypsy as a mentally stunted innocent?
- Or the "grown woman with a taste for married, drug-dealing men" version, which they not only knew about but allegedly encouraged?

You can't have both. If she truly believed she was 14, then the adults "supporting" these relationships were enabling exploitation. If she knew she was an adult, then the infantilization narrative collapses, and the family's own admissions dismantle years of carefully staged victim optics.

What the emails, FOIA records, and post-conviction filings now show is that the Blanchards' public storyline was never about truth, it was about whatever version best served their image in the moment.

Nest Note:

*"She did not fear the lie being exposed.
She feared what would happen if she lost control of it."*

Act 1, Scene 36: Scene of the Crime Reconstruction:

SECTION HEADER: Exhibit C: The Hotel Room & The Walking Girl
FILED BY: Violet Darkly Cawington
FILED UNDER: Violet's Whisper- Reconstructed Notes
REALM: Hybrid- Allegorical - Forensic

Beat 1 ~ Violet Whispers:

Violet speaks with the quiet clarity of someone who has watched too many stories get retold without her consent.

"I saw her.
She walked past me once barefoot.
No limp. No wheelchair.
No shadow of the girl she said she was."

"It was not a miracle.
It was not a healing.
It was a decision."

Beat 2 ~ Reconstruction Notes – 2009 Incident

- Location: VisionCon, Springfield, Missouri
- Found with older male companion
- She abandoned her chair and her exclusive personalized pink Mandalorian costume.
- Stole her mother's money and narcotics. This is a pattern we will see repeating itself.
- Found by name, no fear, no resistance
- Released back into Dee Dee's care without additional review by Kim and David Blanchard. Yes, that same David Blanchard who climbed through the window, "allegedly."

Beat 3 ~ Filed Clue from the Records:

- "Gypsy stated she could walk since age 6. Told boyfriend not to tell anyone."
- *Springfield PD Interview Log, June 2015*

Crow's Note:

"She was not caught in the story. She was directing it."

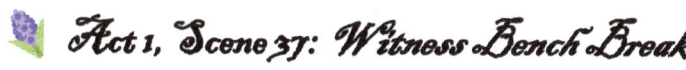
Act 1, Scene 37: Witness Bench Break

SECTION HEADER: Exhibit C: The Hotel Room & The Walking Girl
FILED BY: The Garden of Silent Witnesses
FILED UNDER: Narrative Forensics- Pattern Recognition- Pre-Rewrite Reconstruction
REALM: Allegorical

Where the truth takes tea with the women who remember.

Beat 1 ~ The Motel, the Wheelchair, and the Lie That Learned to Walk

The Garden is dim today.
A storm's coming. But the crows have gathered early.

PETUNIA VERITY CAWINGTON (lighting a match for her testimony candle):
"Well, I always say, when a girl can waltz out of a motel room on her own two feet but ends up back in a wheelchair three days later, someone's writing fiction on hospital letterhead."

RUBY BEGONIA CAWINGTON (adjusting her spectacles, ink-stained fingers twitching):
"I saw the file. It was not Cordelia, The Mourning Orchid, who lied first, it was the girl who said, 'Don't tell anyone I can walk.' That is not a cry for help, this was choreography."

WIDOW RUE (rocking slowly, lace gloves, voice like rust on metal):
"They keep calling it abuse because the truth doesn't fit the dress size. But I knew women like Cordelia. She didn't invent a sickness. She carried it. Fed it. Let it sleep in her bed. And it wasn't hers. It was that child's. And that child made it a costume."

PETUNIA VERITY CAWINGTON (fanning herself):
"Darlin,' that 'ruse' wasn't about a mom fakin' a Syndrome of Stolen Suffering. It was about the girl finally gettin' caught walkin' in Glass Garden. 2011 wasn't a wake-up call. It was a dress rehearsal."

RUBY BEGONIA CAWINGTON:
"And yet they still sold it like a mercy killing. Every TV segment. Every docuseries. Every book with a pink spine and a missing medical file."

WIDOW RUE:
"Mercy's got nothin' to do with it. That girl saw a gene she didn't like and killed the only person still helping her live with it. That was not escaping, but it was erasure."

PETUNIA VERITY CAWINGTON (softly):
"They didn't just bury The Mourning Orchid.
They buried the diagnosis too."

Beat 2 ~ Syndrome of Stolen Suffering (allegorical term for Munchausen by Proxy)

A predatory pattern in which the caregiver steals another's illness identity, crafting and controlling a false narrative of sickness to gain attention, sympathy, or other personal benefit.

In the Garden's parlance, it is the act of plucking the petals of another's pain and wearing them as one's own. While in the real-world courts it is recognized as a severe form of abuse, here in the Garden, it manifests as an invasive vine—rooting in manipulation, fed by deceit, and thriving in the shadows where truth is starved.

Often mistaken for care, it is instead a slow siphoning of life, identity, and credibility from its victim, leaving behind only a withered stem in the public's eye.

Act 1, Scene 38: Choose Your Own Reckoning

SECTION HEADER: Gypsy's Choose Your Own Truth
FILED BY: Fancy Macelli & Amy Mackey
FILED UNDER:
REALM: Forensic

🔀 Beat 1 ~ Choose Your Own Evidence Adventure: What Broke First, The Lie or the Legs?

So, what do you want to believe?

That a girl who walked into a motel room in 2009 was still imprisoned by 2015?
That Dee Dee somehow did not know the wheelchair was a prop... even when her daughter was caught walking out of vision range?
That this was abuse, not ambition?

Because we checked the footage. The files. The fairy tale.
And what we found was not trauma.
It was timing.

You have options now, reader. So, choose carefully.

📄 **OPTION A: Rewind to the Ruse**
🖋 *Return to "Scene, Rewrite, Performance"* to re-examine the interrogation pivot where she did not confess trauma, she cued a new script.
- Pg. 119

🧬 **OPTION B: Follow the Chromosome**
🎈 *Proceed to "The Emotional Core of the Deletion"* to see how the microdeletion unraveled the whole constructed identity and why it had to be silenced.
- Pg. 126

🌸 **OPTION C: Ask the Garden**
🌷 *Visit the Garden of Silent Witnesses- The Soft-Voice Strategy: How a Baby Whisper Became a Bludgeon.* To find out just how a tiny baby voice sold the world a cold blooded murder as a nighttime fairytale.
- Pg. 133

🎭 **OPTION D: Trace the Rewrite**
📖 *Jump to "Through the Hourglass"* to compare timelines and see how every year gained an updated version, and every truth got a costume change.
- Pg. 138

⚖️ **OPTION E: Stay on Trial Path**
📁 *Advance to the next Forensic Segment: "The Emotional Core of the Deletion"*
Where we unmask the gene that would not play along and the story that could not survive its shadow.

📎 *Nest Note:*

"You are not just reading a book.
You are picking which bones to dig up."

Act 1, Scene 39: The Emotional Core of the Deletion

SECTION HEADER: The Diagnosis that Changed the Whole Plot
FILED BY: Fancy Macelli & Amy Mackey
FILED UNDER: Symbolic Distortion- Narrative Psychology- Identity as Strategy
REALM: Forensic

This is not just about what Gypsy omitted.
It is also about what she could not face.

The microdeletion was not just a diagnosis.
It was a contradiction Gypsy could not afford.

To accept it would have meant acknowledging that she was never completely "normal." That she was never going to be the ingenue in a coming-of-age drama where the only obstacle was her mother's leash. That her life, no matter who raised her, was always going to require accommodations, support, and sometimes, limits.

But that does not fit the brand.

The microdeletion stands as proof that she was sick.
That her body, her brain, was different.

And Gypsy does not want that.
She wants to be seen as perfectly capable, endlessly clever, just trapped.
She wants to be the girl who could have done anything... if only someone had let her.

So, she did not deny the microdeletion.
She disappeared it.

The 1q21.1 chromosomal deletion stands in opposition to everything she claims about her story:
— That she could live independently
— That her mind was sharp and her body agile
— That she could have thrived if not for Dee Dee

But the file says otherwise.

She was not a healthy girl imprisoned by a jealous mother.
She was a developmentally delayed woman with real neurological and executive function struggles, struggles confirmed long before a knife was ever lifted.

But the file says otherwise.
She was not held back.
She was already carrying the weight of a chromosomal difference that would have

needed support her entire life.
Not because Dee Dee made her sick,
but because she was already living with a genetic truth she could not rewrite.

This was not a narrative about freedom.
It was a campaign for erasure.
Not of the abuse she claimed... but of the truth that did not flatter her.

Act 1, Scene 40: Musings from the Mind's Morgue

SECTION HEADER: Symbolic Distortion
FILED BY: Fancy Macelli & Amy Mackey
FILED UNDER:
REALM: Forensic

Beat 1 ~ Bone Shard Glossary Entry 7: Symbolic Distortion

Definition: The transformation of inconvenient facts into emotionally charged symbols to justify behavior, redirect blame, or elevate one's perceived suffering. In Gypsy's case, the diagnosis did not just become an oversight it became a metaphorical prison.

Dee Dee did not need to fabricate an illness.
The *existence* of that illness became the betrayal.
And so, she framed the gene itself as the enemy.

She did not challenge the biology.
She removed it entirely from the script.

 ## Nest Note:

"The deletion was never just in the DNA.
It was in the storytelling."

⚖️ Beat 2 ~ Field Notes from the Prosecutor's Desk

- Gypsy did not mention the diagnosis in her confession.
- She did not mention it in early media statements.
- Her legal team omitted it from all public narrative framing.
- And her memoir excludes it entirely despite it being medically central.

This was not an oversight.
It was a conscious tactic to strip away any suggestion that her mother was responding to real medical concerns.

🜂 Beat 3 ~ Narrative Transition

The murder did not happen *despite* her diagnosis.
It happened *in the absence* of it.

She did not kill Dee Dee to escape a fantasy.
She killed her to erase a truth that complicated the myth she wanted to tell.

Because once the world saw the file once they read the diagnosis, saw the impairments, traced the interventions they would stop asking who made her sick… and start wondering why she needed so badly to be seen as well.

🜂 Beat 4 ~ Sealed Evidence - Redacted by Design
The Diagnosis That Did Not Make the Director's Cut

From Lifetime specials to TikTok confessionals, from interviews with Dr. Phil to sit-downs with social media influencers, Gypsy has had no shortage of platforms to rewrite her history. And while she does mention her 1q21.1 microdeletion *briefly* in the print version of *My Time to Stand*, she leaves it out entirely in the audiobook.

That was no accident.
It was a choice. A calculated one.

Because once that gene is named, the lie collapses.
You cannot claim every symptom was fabricated when the deletion exists in your blood.

But on the book tour?
She did not double down on the diagnosis.
She buried it again.

In multiple interviews, Gypsy downplayed any impact of the deletion insisting she was perfectly healthy, untouched by its effects, and wrongly branded by a controlling mother. Then came the claim that her mother was never tested. And the flourish: that her father was tested, and he did not have it. No records. No proof. No citations.

Just vibes.

Meanwhile, extended paternal relatives have shown the exact same cognitive, behavioral, and functional markers associated with 1q21.1. Dee Dee was ruled out in 2011. Geneticists confirmed she was *not* the source.

So why the revision?

Because blaming Dee Dee is easier than facing what the file confirms:
That the gene did not lie.
The brand just did.

 ### Beat 5 ~ Diagnostic Fact:

- 1q21.1 microdeletion is inherited in up to 75% of diagnosed cases
- Dee Dee tested negative via genetic screening at Children's Mercy in 2011.
- No official documentation has ever surfaced proving Rod or Krusty were tested.
- Multiple relatives on Rod's side show signs consistent with mild 1q21.1 presentation.

This is where Gypsy pulls the comment of "I fall in the 75 % of people diagnosed that does not show any symptoms. A test that was never completed. No such case study exists. All she needs to do is look in the mirror and her facial markers tell the truth her mind does not want to accept.

 ### Crow's Note:

"When the DNA didn't cooperate with the script, they rewrote the origin story instead."

Act 1, Scene 41: Voices of the Vines: Petunia's Garden Gavel

SECTION HEADER: Voices of the Vines
FILED BY: Miss Petunia Verity Cawington, Keeper of the Broadcast Roots
FILED UNDER: Garden Testimony - Broadcast Interruptions - Narrative Clarification- Tone Does Not Equal Truth
REALM: Allegorical

"There's something about a girl in a wig and a baby voice that just makes folks forget there's a body on the floor."

Petunia here. And I am pulling the gavel out for just a second, because we need to talk about something real plain:

🕯 *The truth does not always scream. But sometimes it sings lullabies while hiding a knife.*

When Gypmydia narrates her story like a deconstructed Happily Never After Studios episode—with that saccharine lilt, the carefully measured tears, the wide-eyed bewilderment, you are not watching trauma processing.

You are watching trauma *production*.

This is not an aftershock. It is a rehearsal.

She is not "finding her voice."
She is *casting herself in the lead role.*

"Delusion pruned. Lies composted. We bloom in facts now. You may now return to the spectacle already in progress."

Act 1, Scene 42: The Soft-Voice Strategy: How a Baby Whisper Became a Bludgeon

SECTION HEADER: Emotional Alchemy - Narrative Disguise Tactics
FILED BY: Fancy Macelli - Narrative Analyst Division
FILED UNDER: Memory Laundering - Rhetorical Weaponry - Docuseries Deception
REALM: Forensic + Media Myth making

Beat 1 ~ Clinical Cue: Memory Laundering Through Performance

Her baby-talk delivery is not a trauma tic. It is a rhetorical weapon.
Psychologists refer to this tactic as **memory laundering**—a process by which emotionally or legally risky memories are softened, reshaped, and retold in more socially acceptable packaging.
It is a protective layer.
It shields her not from what was done to her but from what she did.
She does not relive the murder.
She retells it like it's *Goodnight Moon* with an indictment.

 Beat 2 ~ The Gene That Got the Guillotine

And let's not lose the thread, crows.
Because this fairytale filter
does not just coat the murder, it coats the medicine.
The moment she steps into the spotlight, the **gene vanishes**.
The deletion disorder? Gone.
Dee Dee's extensive, documented medical history?
Scrubbed like a chalkboard before opening night.
It is not a coincidence.
It is not trauma.
IT'S A SCRIPT.

🎭 Beat 3 ~ Media Moment: Direction by Docuseries

Let's be honest, HBO knew what they were doing.
So did Hulu.
So did the podcast producers, the documentary editors, and every platform that laid a twinkling piano track under a confession to murder.

"Lights up on a wheelchair.
Fade in the voice-over.
Cue the ukulele music."
Mainstream media did not just allow the infantilized tone to stand.

They choreographed it.
They wrapped a criminal conspiracy in a cashmere monologue and called it survival.

📖 Beat 4 ~ Crow's Note: How to Spot a Performed Narrative

Next time you hear a true crime narration whispered like a bedtime story, pause.
Ask yourself:

- Who benefits from this tone?
- Does the delivery match the content?
- What part of the story is being replaced by sweetness?
  If the answer is "no one ever asked,"
  you are not listening to truth.
  You are watching a puppet show with the blood rinsed off.

🎯 Beat 5 ~ Final Strike: Not a Fairytale. A Fraud.

Gypsy Rose is not confused about what happened.
She is relying on the rest of us being confused about who she was when it happened.
That tone? That "little girl lost" performance?
It does not come from healing.
It comes from **marketing**.
This is not *Madeline in Paris*.
It is **Methadone in Missouri**.
And love, it is not the truth.
It is the prettiest lie that ever got a book deal.

📒 Filed. Feathered. And one hell of a performance.

📄 Beat 6 ~ Bone Shard Glossary Entry 8:

Memory Laundering (n.)
A psychological and rhetorical tactic in which a speaker reshapes emotionally or legally dangerous memories into softened, socially acceptable narratives, often through tone, metaphor, or selective omission.

Frequently used to:
- Reduce personal culpability
- Evoke audience sympathy
- Reframe criminal behavior as misunderstood suffering

Example:

Recounting a murder in the tone of a bedtime story to appear less threatening and more "childlike."

Note:
Memory laundering is **not** a symptom of trauma, it is a **strategy of performance**, often reinforced by media coaching, narrative rehearsals, or post-hoc branding efforts.

🪶 **Filed in:** Emotional Alchemy – Symbolic Distortion – Narrative Omission Strategy

♥ Act 1, Scene 43: Closing the First Door: Reflections Beyond the Mirror

SECTION HEADER: Emotional Alchemy - Narrative Disguise Tactics
FILED BY: Fancy Macelli & Amy Mackey
FILED UNDER: Performed Innocence - Preformed Sickness - Docuseries Deception
REALM: Forensic + Media Myth making

🪶 Beat 1 ~ Mack: "Lies do not grow in a vacuum. They take root in silence."

I used to think the loudest parts of this case were the scariest, the confessions, the headlines, the blood...the medical abuse.
But it is the quiet parts that haunt me.
The gaps. The contradictions.
The eerie precision with which Gypsy shaped her own myth
and the chilling silence that followed each rewrite.

She did not just perform sickness.
She performed innocence.
And the world seemed hungry for a villain they could bury and a girl they could save.

I scrubbed through hours of footage.
Hundreds of pages of sealed records.
And beneath every contradiction was a pattern.

One built not on pain, but on power.
The kind of power that comes from being underestimated.
The kind of power the world gives you when it feels sorry for you.

Gypsy's lies just kept getting better.

🌿 Beat 2 ~ A Weed from the Garden

"She did not run from danger. She ran the narrative."

We watched from beneath the floorboards of her fairytale,
buried in mulch and memory.
She did not flee into safety;
she fled into storytelling.
And when the petals started to fall,
she plucked them herself
and blamed the wind.

We saw how she rehearsed her lines.
How she softened the sharpest truths with powdered sugar.
And how the world leaned in, not because they were fooled,
but because they liked the flavor better that way.

Truth does not vanish on its own.
It gets buried.
In sympathy.
In performance.
In perfect lighting and practiced tears.

She did not rewrite history.
She restaged it.

Beat 3 ~ Fancy: Every performance has a price. I just kept the receipts."

I did not come into this expecting to be a forensic archivist of lies.
I came in believing the version they sold:
The girl in the wheelchair.
The mother with a diagnosis.
The murderer no one questioned.

But what I found was not a tragedy.
It was theater.
A script so well-rehearsed, even the media forgot to ask for a second draft.

Dee Dee was buried without a defense.
Nick was tried without mercy.
And Gypsy?
She was handed a spotlight.

I do not care how many Facebook posts or Netflix specials call her brave what she did was calculated.
I have read the files.
I have tracked the contradictions.
I have watched how sympathy turned into strategy.

And when you realize how far that lie has traveled,
how many people it trampled on the way to a book deal,
you do not forget.

They want you to see her as a girl who broke free.
But I see the woman who staged her escape and curated the applause.

Act 1, Scene 44: Through the Hourglass – The Myth of the Mutable Self

SECTION HEADER: The Ruse Was Up
FILED BY: Fancy Macelli & Amy Mackey
FILED UNDER: Timeline Weaponization
REALM: Forensic

Beat 1 ~ Rebuttal to Quote 4: "The ruse was up."

But which ruse? What ended, exactly? And if it was over... why did the performance escalate?

If the ruse ended, why did the lies keep multiplying?

"It's no use going back to yesterday, because I was a different person then."
- *Lewis Carroll, Through the Looking-Glass*

In Wonderland, time does not tick.
It slips sideways.
It forgets what it knew and becomes what it needed to be.

For Gypsy Rose Blanchard, time itself became a weapon.
She did not just live inside a broken clock,
she rewound it whenever the truth got too close.

And when she said, "the ruse was up"?
She was not ending a deception.
She was launching a new one.

 **Nest Note:**

"She did not run out of time.
She rewrote the timeline."

The story she sold us, of years locked away, isolated, controlled,
was not just exaggerated.
It was impossible.

The FOIA documents, police records, witness interviews, and medical logs reveal a remarkably different timeline:

Year	Reality	Gypsy's Later Fantasy
2009–2010	Make-A-Wish trips, VisionCon appearances, Disney photos	"Imprisoned in a house with jingle bells von the doors"
2011	Online dating, older boyfriends, public conventions	"No access to the outside world"
212–2013	Shoplifting with Dee Dee, travel for charity	"Forced crimes under captivity"
214	Secret grooming of Nick Godejohn online	"Isolated and helpless, waiting to be saved"
2015	Unsupervised phone calls, planning murder	"Trapped, with no way out but death"

The facts did not change.
Only the hourglass did.

Each time Gypsy spun the latest version of her life,
the grains of sand rearranged into a prettier picture.

Beat 2 ~ The Tricks of Her Timeline:

- Public outings recast as "forced charity events."
- Online dating reframed as "secret cries for help."
- Walks and travel erased with "I didn't know I could."
- Planning murder recast as "escape from abuse."

She did not lose track of time.
She bent it.
Because in Gypsy's Wonderland, time was only real if it served the story.

 ## Crow's Note:

"Memory does not blur by accident.
In Wonderland, even the clocks lie when it is convenient."

The hourglass did not run out.
It was flipped.
Repeatedly
until yesterday's lie became today's gospel.
And no one remembered how many versions came before.

Because by the time the glass cracked,
the audience had already decided which way the sand should fall.

Act 1, Scene 45: Myth Maintenance Panel: Six Impossible Selves Before Breakfast

SECTION HEADER: Softened Narratives
FILED BY: Fancy Macelli & Amy Mackey
FILED UNDER: Softened Narratives – Interchangeable Personas
REALM: Forensic

"Why, sometimes I've believed as many as six impossible things before breakfast."
– *The White Queen, Through the Looking-Glass*

She did not just change the story.
She **multiplied** it.

Each recent version of herself softened the edge of what she had done.
Each new telling drifted further from reality
and deeper into mythology.

 **Nest Note:**

"She did not bury the truth.
She dressed it up for another encore."

Persona	What She Claimed	What the Records Show
🧸 The Helpless Child	"I didn't know better."	Secret online activity, travel, grooming
🎭 The Prisoner	"I was trapped."	Attended events, traveled, dated
🎭 The Innocent Accomplice	"Nick did everything."	She started planning, directed thefts, did instructional videos
🩺 The Forced Patient	"My mom made me sick."	1q21.1 deletion confirmed
🖼️ The Misunderstood Daughter	"I tried to tell."	No reports filed, active coverups
🏰 The Survivor Princess	"I escaped captivity."	No locks, no alarms, no isolation

Each persona earned her a new kind of sympathy
and pushed the murder further into the shadows.

 **Crow's Note:**

"The most dangerous kind of liar isn't the one who fools the world—it's the one who first fools herself."

In Wonderland, six impossible things before breakfast was a game.
In Gypsy's world, it was **a marketing plan**.
The truth did not survive breakfast.
The story did.

Act 1, Scene 46: Mirror of Many Selves

SECTION HEADER: Lies & Contradictions
FILED BY: Fancy Macelli & Amy Mackey
FILED UNDER: Changing Timelines– Public Life Distortion
REALM: Forensic

"Who in the world am I? Ah, that is the great puzzle."
- *Alice's Adventures in Wonderland*

She did not just change the timeline.
She changed herself,
again and again,
to match the audience standing in front of her mirror.

Platform	Gypsy's Claim	Contradiction
2015 Interrogation	"I wanted to be free."	No mention of abuse; clear motive
216 Court Hearing	"I was afraid and confused."	Assertive legal strategy
217 Dr. Phil	"She made me lie."	Sex chats, cosplay, manipulation clear
219 The Endless Story Channel Film	"I was a prisoner."	Documented public life
224 Memoir	"I was trained to act sick."	Proven medical diagnosis, contradictions

---

 Nest Note:

"She was not misremembering.
She was rehearsing."

Each revision pulled her further from the knife.
Further from motive.
Further from reality.

Until the echo of her voice
sounded more real than the evidence ever could.

This was not trauma fog.
This was **myth maintenance**.

🪓 Act 1 scene 47: From the Ashes Mini-Series: Sympathy's a Hell of a Drug

SECTION HEADER: Pill Popping Persona
FILED BY: Fancy Macelli & Amy Mackey
FILED UNDER: Quotes of Complete Lies- Posthumous Defamation
REALM: Forensic

⬛ Beat 1 ~ Gypsy Rose and the Pill-Popping Persona She Blamed on Her Mother

🔖 **Quote 5:** "She claims Dee Dee kept her pills locked in a safe, then says she found them lying around. So, which is it?"

🧠 Beat 2 ~ Narrative Setup: "I Was Addicted to Pain Pills"

Gypsy has long claimed that part of her abuse included forced sedation. In interviews, in her memoir, and in her most dramatic performances, she alleges that Dee Dee crushed up pain pills and put them into her feeding tube so she would appear cognitively and developmentally delayed.

According to her, this is why she could not tell the truth during the infamous CPS visit. It is a powerful image, this innocent girl drugged into silence. A child rendered pliant, blurred, and confused by a mother with medical authority and a twisted agenda.

Sounds shocking,
until you read the records.

Because the truth, once again, is not that Gypsy was overmedicated.
It is that she was overacting.
What she sells as drugged compliance was a carefully cultivated excuse. A story that shifts every time she needs a little more sympathy.

And the contradiction at the center of this chapter is the claim that Dee Dee both tightly locked up her medication and simultaneously left them scattered beneath old costumes? Again, Gypsy is a storyteller building her brand.

📁 Beat 3 ~ What the Records Actually Show

Let us start with the CPS visit, the moment Gypsy most often references as proof she was too sedated to tell the truth.

She claims Dee Dee drugged her before the social worker arrived. That she was foggy, slow, and too afraid to speak.

But here is the problem with that:
Dee Dee did not know CPS was coming.

There was no advance warning.
No phone call.
No tip-off.
Just a surprise visit.

And when CPS arrived?

- They spoke to Gypsy **alone**
- They found her to be **verbal, pleasant, and alert**
- They noted some developmental delay but not enough to trigger intervention
- Dee Dee provided an ID and birth certificate showing Gypsy was over 18

If Gypsy had truly been drugged to the point of mental fog, it would have shown.

But it did not.

There is no documentation of sedation.
No slurred speech.
No inability to answer simple questions.
No red flags that would signal a child being held hostage by narcotics.

This was not a girl sedated into submission.
It was a girl spinning a story long after the fact because it served her better than the truth.

And if Dee Dee were so controlling, so paranoid, so precise...
why would she have left opioids out in the open for Gypsy to "find under a pile of costumes"?

The contradiction collapses on contact.
You do not lock the safe and leave the key in the candy dish.
And you do not scatter Schedule II narcotics around a child's bedroom while claiming to control her every move.

The reality is: Gypsy used this narrative pivot to explain away her own theft, her own dependency, and her own escalating manipulation.

🧪 Beat 4 ~ Timeline Inconsistencies: The "Found the Pills" Fairytale

Gypsy's story about pain pills is not just inconsistent it is self-contradictory.

In one interview, she says Dee Dee kept her medications locked in a safe.

In another, she claims she found pills "under a pile of costumes" in her bedroom.

You cannot have both. But she sure tired.

If Dee Dee was strict and controlling with prescriptions as Gypsy claims in her own book, then the idea that powerful opioids were just lying around like forgotten Halloween candy makes no sense.

This is not just a narrative inconsistency.
It's a pivot point.
A constructed loophole designed to justify what came next: theft, addiction, and a murder that was not as sudden or helpless as she now portrays.

Because when you track the timeline?

💊 Beat 5 ~ Documented Pattern of Pill Theft

Gypsy did not just find pills. She took them intentionally and repeatedly according to her despite there is no proof to back this claim up except one little ER visit. There is a story there and don't worry we are about to tell it. Sources say that Gypsy ran away starting at 11 years old however this is the only timeline we have been able to verify with outside sources.

1. **2009:** First known attempt at running away. She abandoned her wheelchair and snuck off to have hot Star Wars sex in her pink costume from the Mandalorian movie, with an unidentified Storm Trooper. She left with narcotics and stole money from Dee Dee's purse.
2. **2011:** Second alleged "runaway" attempt.
   She left home with both cash and pills. This was not a frantic escape. It was a deliberate looting.
3. **2013:** Second attempt. Same pattern. Same MO. More pills gone.
4. **2015:** Post-murder, pre-arrest. Before she left the house, she packed her mom's medications. Dee Dee's body was still warm, and Gypsy made sure she had her fix.

None of this fits the narrative of a sedated victim.

It fits the pattern of a manipulator preparing for the next chapter, long before the last one had ended.

Gypsy's addiction was not to pills.
It was to pity.

And the story she tells about finding those pills under a pile of costumes.

We have stagecraft roleplaying evidence.

🏥 Beat 6 ~ Eyewitness Account: The Emergency Room Threat

One Springfield resident recalled a disturbing encounter at a local ER.

She and her daughter were receiving care in a curtained-off bay.

In the next bay over?
Gypsy Rose Blanchard.

The woman described Gypsy as aggressive demanding pain medication, insisting she needed it, and escalating her threats when told no.

She reportedly turned to the doctor and said:

"If you don't get me what I want, I'll tell them you touched me."

The hospital staff did not hear it.
But the witness did.

This was not 2015.
This was **years before the murder**.

Gypsy did not suddenly become manipulative after the crime.
She had years of practice.

She did not invent lies to survive.
She used them to control.

Beat 7 ~ The Truth About Dee Dee's Pain

Dee Dee had a severe foot injury.
She almost lost that foot.
She walked with difficulty, bore chronic pain, and needed medical management to function.

That included pain medication prescribed by doctors, monitored across providers, and tightly controlled in the home.

Because pills like that?

They are not casual.

They are locked away.
Logged.
Watched.
Tracked.

Especially in homes where there is another vulnerable person, like a teenager with a history of manipulation.

Dee Dee was not hoarding drugs to play puppet master.
She was managing a household with complex medical demands and trying to function through injury.

What did Gypsy do?

She reframed her mother's condition into villainy.

She took what was not hers.
She blamed the dead.
And then she said:

"I was addicted because of her."

Except…

- 🧬 There were no withdrawal symptoms at the time of arrest.
- 🧬 No detox period needed in jail.
- 🧬 No medical alerts, complications, or emergencies.

She was not detoxing from pain meds.

She was detoxing from attention.

🐷 Beat 8 ~ Sympathy Baiting, Disney-Style

In interviews, Gypsy often cries about being "forced" to smile, to wear costumes, to take pictures at Disney World.

She frames it as a trauma.

"I was made to act happy when I wasn't."

Let's talk about that.

The Disney footage tells a different story:

- She is dancing on Main Street USA.
- She is going at those Royal Mashed Potatoes like the palace just declared carbs do not count.
- She is hugging characters, laughing, posing for cameras.
- She is receiving free toys, meals, and VIP treatment through charity organizations.
- She is actively engaging in interviews with the media.

No sign of sedation.
No visible distress.
Just a girl performing and enjoying the applause.

But in her retelling, those moments become a cage.
The smiles become shackles.
The theme parks become prison cells.

Because if she can paint the happiest moments as suffering, then everything else must seem unbearable by comparison.

Beat 9 ~ Final Crow's Note

Gypsy did not lose control of her life.
She took it from the one person still holding it together.

And she blamed the pills.
She blamed the press.
She blamed the pain.

All while collecting sympathy like it was candy.
Because in her version?

Stealing medication was survival.
Lying to doctors was defense.
And dancing at Disney?

Well, that was just another form of abuse.

But if she really believed any of that,
why did she keep the costume?

Why did she keep the story going?

Because the performance was not over.
And the next act?
Was murder.

💀 Act 1, Scene 48: Bone Shard Glossary Entry 8: Myth Maintenance

SECTION HEADER: Bone Shard Glossary Entry
FILED BY: Fancy Macelli & Amy Mackey
FILED UNDER: Bone Shard Glossary Entry
REALM: Forensic

Beat 1 ~ Myth Maintenance

Definition:
Myth Maintenance refers to the conscious or unconscious process of updating a personal narrative to better align with public expectations, emotional needs, or branding goals.

In Gypsy's case, each retelling of her story reinforced her innocence and victimhood while distancing her from the act of murder. Regardless of how much prior evidence contradicted those new versions.

A lie that evolves becomes harder to trace.
And a lie that has rewarded?
Becomes a lifestyle.

Beat 2 ~ In Context – Pill Contradiction

She says Dee Dee kept her pills in a locked safe.
Then she says she found them "under a pile of costumes."

She claims she was too sedated to speak to CPS.
But the records say she was verbal, pleasant, and alert.

Crow's Note

"They say liars need good memories.
But Gypsy did not need memory
she had media.

She did not revise the story in secret.
She revised it on camera.
In documentaries.
In interviews.
In ghostwritten memoirs.

And when the cracks showed
the world rushed to glue them shut with pity."

● Nest Note

"She was not misremembering.
She was rehearsing.
And every time the audience clapped,
she wrote a new encore."

📎 Beat 3 ~ Sidebar: Narrative Evolution or Deliberate Revision?

Between 2015 and 224, Gypsy's story did not just grow more dramatic.
It grew more strategic.

While trauma can affect memory,
her pivots were consistently timed,
always toward more innocence, more helplessness, more sympathy.

These are the same techniques we see in:

- Cult leaders
- Celebrity grifters
- Strategic defendants

🔑 Act 1, Scene 49: The Poison They Preferred

SECTION HEADER: The Lies She Shouted
FILED BY: Fancy Macelli & Amy Mackey
FILED UNDER: Softened Narratives – Interchangeable Personas
REALM: Forensic

💬 "Curiouser and curiouser!" - Alice

Some lies are shouted.
Others are whispered,
gently repackaged until they become gospel.
Gypsy's new identity,
Survivor.
Scapegoat.
Misunderstood girl
was not born in the interrogation room.
It was born in the visitation room of Greene County Jail.
Reinforced by reporters.
Repackaged by handlers.
Fed back to her until she believed it, too.
This was not healing.
It was branding therapy.

🔒 Beat 1 ~ Keys to the Lie #1: Narrative Self-Enhancement (Bone Shard Glossary Entry 8)

Term: Narrative Self-Enhancement
Definition: The act of reshaping one's identity or life story to protect self-image, especially when the truth is painful, shameful, or incriminating.
In Context:
Instead of confronting the truth about premeditation, Gypsy reshaped the narrative:
From planner - to pawn
From participant - to product
From murderer - to martyr
But She did not rewrite the story because it was not true.
She rewrote it because the truth wasn't useful anymore.

❇ She told the versions that made her feel better.
And the media told the versions that made her look better.
Gypsy's new identity was curated through:
• Selective storytelling
• Therapist reframing

- Media grooming
- Fanbase reinforcement

It felt emotionally real.
But "felt" and "was" not the same thing.

Gypsy's turning her guilt into gold.

🔒 Beat 2 ~ Keys to the Lie #2: Emotional Alibi (Bone Shard Glossary Entry 9)

Term: Emotional Alibi
Definition: The strategic use of emotional vulnerability or trauma cues to deflect accountability and elicit sympathy.
In Context:
Every time Gypsy cried, confessed, or paused just long enough for her voice to crack, she built a new alibi.
Not for the crime.
For the motive.
Her feelings became her defense.
And they worked.
She did not deny the knife.
She just cried until you forgot it was in her hand.

🎨 Act 1 Scene 50: Painting the Roses Red

SECTION HEADER: Musical Interlude
FILED BY: Fancy Macelli & Amy Mackey
FILED UNDER: Never Questioned Contradictions – Shifting Stories- Rebrand of Murder
REALM: Hybrid Forensic & Allegorical

> 💬 *"Sentence first - verdict afterwards!" - The Queen of Hearts*

🎵 Beat 1 ~ Painting The Roses Red
by Kathryn Beaumont and The Mellomen · 1951

Bum bum bum bum.
Painting the roses red.
We're painting the roses red.
We dare not stop,
Or waste a drop,
So let the paint be spread.
We're painting the roses reeeed.
We're painting the roses red.
Oh, painting the roses red.
And many a tear be shed,
Because we know,
They'll cease to grow,
In fact, they'll soon be dead,
NOOOOO...
And yet we go ahead,
Painting the roses red.
Painting the roses red.
We're painting the roses red.
Oh pardon me,
But Mister Three,
Why must you paint them red?
(Huh?)
(Oooooh!)
(Well, the fact is Miss we planted the white roses by mistake and...)
The Queen she likes 'em red,
If she saw white instead,
She'd raise a fuss,
And each of us,
Would quickly loose his head!
(Goodness)
Since this is the part we dread,

We're painting the roses red.
(Oh dear! Well, then let me help you!)
Painting the roses red.
We're painting the roses red.
Don't tell the Queen,
What you have seen,
Or say that's what we said,
But we're painting the roses red.
Yes, painting the roses red.
Not pink.
Not green.
Not aquamarine.
We're painting the roses red.

Beat 2 ~ Surface Symbolism (in the story itself)

- Covering a mistake – The gardeners planted the wrong roses (white instead of red) and are now frantically covering it up rather than fixing the root problem.
- Fear-driven compliance – The Queen's wrath (and threat of execution) forces everyone to pretend, rather than admit fault.
- Artificial perfection – Beauty and order are maintained through deception, not truth, red roses aren't grown, they're painted.

Beat 3 ~ Deeper Symbolism in a Broader Context

1. Appearance Over Reality
   - The act of painting is a metaphor for hiding inconvenient truths with a cosmetic fix.
   - It's a performance of normalcy and beauty designed to please authority or the public eye, even when the core is false.
2. Authoritarian Control & Fear
   - The Queen symbolizes unchecked authority, her preferences dictate reality, even if they defy logic or nature.
   - The gardeners' survival depends on deception, showing how systems of fear produce false narratives.
3. Futility & Destruction
   - "They'll cease to grow / In fact, they'll soon be dead" is key. Altering the surface destroys the natural life beneath.
   - It's a commentary on how covering up truth often kills the integrity of what it hides.

Beat 4 ~ In Your Garden Allegory

-The Roses - Truth, evidence, or authentic memory.

-White Roses - The unaltered reality (possibly inconvenient or unprofitable for those in control).

- Red Paint - Narrative manipulation, media spin, false diagnoses, or rewritten history.

- The Queen - The narrative authority - media networks, co-authors, prosecutors, demanding a particular version of events.

- The Gardeners - Those who enable the lie out of fear or self-preservation (family, collaborators, opportunists).

In this frame, "painting the roses red" mirrors exactly what we've been documenting: altering the story so it fits the preferred narrative, even if the alteration is obvious, harmful, and kills the original truth.

Beat 5 ~ The Repaint That Was Never Questioned

The contradictions were never questioned.
They were **repainted**.
Every time Gypsy's story shifted,
the media did not hesitate.
They shifted with her.
They added violins.
Softened the lighting.
Rewrote the script with trembling hands and hungry pens.
- HBO called it *heartbreaking*
- Lifetime called it *bravery*
- Buzzfeed called it *viral*
- Stanfield called it *strategy*
- Kristy Blanchard called it *branding*

And no one...
no one...
called it what it was:
a campaign.

 Garden Gossip

They did not fix the gaps.
They planted flowers over the graves.

Every version of Gypsy's myth was not exposed.
It was celebrated.
Cultivated.
Watered with sympathy until it bloomed into legend.
Because the press was not interested in breaking the illusion.
They were too busy painting the roses red.

🌷 "It did not matter how many petals fell away.
The vines of her story kept growing,
choking the truth until only beauty remained."

 *Act 1, Scene 51: Whisper on the Wind*

SECTION HEADER: Anatomy of a Lie
FILED BY: Fancy Macelli & Amy Mackey
FILED UNDER: Media Allies- Legal Teams- Fake Fans
REALM: Forensic

Beat 1 ~ Anatomy of a Lie

Each narrative shift was amplified by:
- Media allies
- Legal teams
- Facebook fan groups

Not one of these shifts corresponded to new evidence.
The FOIA files did not change.
The police reports did not change.
The autopsy did not change.
Only the performance did

This was narrative cultivation.
And Wonderland,
never questions a rose
painted the right shade of red.

Act 1 Forensic Suite

🕯️ Act 1, Scene 52: Bone Shard Glossary Entries- Anatomy of a Myth

A forensic autopsy of the narratives that sold, the performances that spread, and the lies that calcified.

SECTION HEADER: Forensic Suite
FILED BY: Fancy Macelli & Amy Mackey
FILED UNDER: Never Questioned Contradictions – Shifting Stories- Rebrand of Murder
REALM: Forensic

💀 Beat 1 ~ Bone Shard Glossary Entry: Myth Maintenance

She did not just misremember,
she curated.
Every retelling became another draft, sanded, reshaped, focus-grouped for sympathy.
This was not a story smudged by trauma.
It was a lie sanded to a mirror polish.

📌 Crow's Whisper:

"She did not need a good memory. She had good editors."

💀 Beat 2~ Bone Shard Glossary Entry: Narrative Self-Enhancement

Each edit erased a little more guilt.
Gypsy's story was not *recovered memory*; it was more like *refined messaging*.
When a timeline threatened her image, it disappeared.
When a contradiction surfaced, it was reframed.

🩸 Forensic Echo:

The motive did not change.
The script did.

💀 Beat 3~ Bone Shard Glossary Entry: Emotional Alibi

She did not deny the knife.
She just cried until we forgot she held it.

The media bought it.
The court bent toward it.
And we, collectively mistook emotion for evidence.

 Garden Gossip:

"It is not that the jury did not hear the truth.
They just could not hear it over the violins."

 Beat 4 ~ Bone Shard Glossary Entry: Social Role Reinforcement

Definition:
A defense built not on facts, but on the strategic performance of vulnerability. It does not dispute the act itself — the knife remains in hand — but floods the scene with enough visible sorrow to make the blade disappear from memory.

This alibi blooms when emotion is mistaken for exoneration: when tears sway the media, soften the court, and drown the truth beneath a soundtrack of sympathy. The violins play, the audience leans in, and the evidence fades into the background.

Every applause taught her the next line.
Gypsy did not discover the helpless act overnight.
She learned it, through every "poor baby," every Facebook like, every news anchor who wept on cue.

She was rewarded for the character.
So, she stayed in costume.

 Nest Note:

"She was not pretending to be a survivor.
She was learning how to *market* one."

 Beat 5 ~ Garden Glossary Entry: Botanical Truth Syndrome

Definition:
A condition where surface beauty is cultivated to conceal the decay beneath. Like flowers blooming over a grave, it thrives on aesthetic camouflage: the shaved head, the whispery voice, the wide eyes, all designed to perfume the petals so no one notices the blood in the roots.

It is the art of narrative horticulture: masking guilt or manipulation with sweetness, softness, and carefully curated vulnerability. In the Garden, it is often diagnosed when truth is smothered under layers of performative innocence, leaving only the appearance of purity while the soil itself rots unseen

She did not smell like guilt.
She smelled like sugar.
The shaved head.
The whispery voice.
The wide eyes.
Camouflage.
And like flowers blooming over a grave, her aesthetic masked the rot.

🌷 *Violet's Warning:*
"They perfumed the petals, so no one noticed the blood in the roots."

Act 1, Scene 53: "Unlearning the Lie" Workbook Prompt

SECTION HEADER: Forensic Suite
FILED BY: Fancy Macelli & Amy Mackey
FILED UNDER: Workbook Preview
REALM: Forensic

Activity 1.0: How Many Victims Were in the Room?

Before we wrap this phase of the story, sit with the questions no one in the courtroom ever asked:

- Rewatch Gypsy's 2015 interrogation.
- Re-read her early interviews.
- Watch how the story shapeshifts, how quickly, and how conveniently.

✎ Use the matching journal prompt in your *Unlearning the Lie*™ workbook or download the printable version from the **Bones & Prompts appendix** at the end of this book.

Reflect:

1. What were the three major shifts in Gypsy's story from arrest to memoir?
2. What public reactions did each version provoke?
3. Which facts were buried, ignored, or outright contradicted?
4. Who gained power, sympathy, or money from each transformation?

Because in Wonderland, every narrative is a house of cards,
and the ones who shuffle the deck always bet you will never look too closely.

 Act 1, Scene 54: Illusions of the Innocent

SECTION HEADER: Forensic Suite
FILED BY: Fancy Macelli & Amy Mackey
FILED UNDER: Comparative Studies
REALM: Forensic

 *Ink of Mourning:*
"All that we see or seem is but a dream within a dream."
- Edgar Allan Poe

Beat 1 ~ Real World Comparisons

Throughout this book, we will be drawing comparisons to other real-world cases, stories that echo, reflect, or unravel the same narrative mechanics we see in Gypsy's rise to myth. These are not detours. They are diagnostic.

Jennifer Pan's case is one such mirror.

Before we meet Jennifer Pan in full, let us pause.
Because this chapter is not just about Gypsy.
It is about the pattern she stands for.

But before we step fully into her story, we need to hold up the one Gypsy offered us and study how it was built. Because what Gypsy performed was not just deception. It was *narrative rehearsal*.

Each retelling tested a new script:
- Trauma as a performance cue.
- Victimhood as a costume.
- Suffering as an act that demanded applause.

And the audience?
We rewarded her for it.

 Beat 2 ~ Parallel Performance: Gypsy & Jennifer Pan

Jennifer Pan did not walk into court as a monster.
She walked in as a daughter:

- Soft voice.
- Polite demeanor.
- A tragic backstory woven with trembling hands.

She cried on the stand.
She spoke of fear.
She painted her parents as cruel, controlling obstacles.

The public leaned in.
The jury did not.

Because what Jennifer created was not just a lie.
It was a **calculated identity**,
one that bent the facts until they fit her emotional alibi.

And the moment her parents stopped being useful to her story,
she planned their deaths.

 Beat 3 ~ Bone Shard Glossary Entry 14: Fantasy Rehearsal

Definition:
The psychological process of imagining, scripting, and emotionally preparing for future scenarios, often blending fiction and reality to reduce guilt or amplify a sense of control.

In Context:
Gypsy rehearsed her survival story long before the crime.
Through cosplay.
Through character chats.
Through trauma fiction that made rebellion feel like rescue.

"She did not commit a crime in the moment. She auditioned for it for years."

 Beat 4 ~ Fragment from the Files

"I feel like I've lived so many lives. But none of them were mine."

This quote is self-scripting.
She was not lost in her identity.

She was constructing it
out of fragments, fandoms, and falsehoods.

Beat 5 ~ Crime Board Snapshot: Jennifer Pan vs. Gypsy Rose Blanchard

Trait	Jennifer Pan	Gypsy Rose Blanchard
Double Life	Faked university & work	Online cosplay, secret boyfriends
Claim of Abuse	Parents were too controlling	Mother was abusive & manipulative
Murder Motive	Wanted freedom from control	Claimed escape from abuse
Evidence of Planning	Burner phones, notes, staged 911 call	Nick grooming, cosplay plans, surveillance
Public Reception	Vilified, sentenced	Sympathized with, celebrated
Court Outcome	Life sentence	10 years, paroled at 8
Media Portrayal	None	Star of films, books, and social media

🌷 Act 1, Scene 55: *Garden of Silent Witnesses*

SECTION HEADER: Court of Painted Roses Intermission
FILED BY: Petunia Verity Cawington
FILED UNDER: A Deeper Meaning
REALM: Allegorical

Beat 1 ~ The flowers heard it all and they chose silence."

When Gypmydia began spinning her myth of captivity and helplessness, she was not doing it in a vacuum.

There were witnesses.
There were friends.
There were family members.
There were doctors, nurses, neighbors, classmates, and charity organizers, all of whom saw the cracks in the image she portrayed.

They saw her walk when she thought no one was looking.
They heard her laugh in parking lots, free and vibrant.
They watched her flirt, shop, cosplay, scheme.
They read the petal messages that did not match the trembling voice she used on stage.

And yet,
they said nothing.
Or worse, they excused it.

In Wonderland, silence is not innocence.
It is complicity.
The garden was not fooled.
It was simply too enchanted to resist the lie.

 *Tiger-Lily's Note:*

"Even a flower with thorns can pretend not to notice the blood it blooms in."

Beat 2 ~ Petals That Bleed

"The most beautiful gardens often hide the deepest wounds."

The Garden wept when Gypmydia spun her story of survival.
But no one wept for Cordelia.
Not when she was alive.
Not when she was brutally murdered.

Because when sympathy gardens are tended,
only the flowers that fit the story are allowed to bloom.

Cordelia's family abandoned her memory long before the grave.
Ten years in a box.
No urn.
No marker.
Just silence.

And even now, that urn sits empty.

Because grieving The Mourning Orchid would mean confronting the lie.
And that is a garden no one wants to walk through.

 *Violet Mourns:*
"They painted over her thorns with red and called it healing. But even the petals knew what they were hiding."

Act 1, Scene 56: Letters from the Gallows

SECTION HEADER: Personal Reflections
FILED BY: Fancy Macelli & Amy Mackey
FILED UNDER: Thoughts & Grievances
REALM: Forensic & Allegorical

Beat 1 ~ Mack's Caws for Consideration

Reading Through the Role

"Some lies are lullabies. They do not scream. They sing softly until you are too enchanted to ask if they are true."

The first time I watched Gypsy's interrogation, it hit me. Not because of what she said, but because of what she didn't say, no mention of DeeDee being an abusive mom, not once! No abuse of any kind! She was calm, cute and flirty. And let's not forget her saying repeatedly, "I would never hurt my mama, my mama is my best friend."

But that version of her disappeared fast. In its place came styling, spin, and a carefully rehearsed script of abuse and innocence.

That was the moment I knew: this was not a case of confusion. It was a performance. She did not perform pain, she performed purity. And the public rewarded it.

Because what is easier? Confronting the possibility that a woman who looks like a victim might also be the architect of a murder? Or clapping anyway because the mascara was running just, right?

I believed the lie too. I think we all did.

It felt obvious... until it didn't. Until I realized something simple but devastating in that first interrogation, the one that mattered, she never mentioned abuse. Not once. Not when it would have counted.

And yet, years later, that is the story she sold. That is the script Kristy, Melissa, The Endless Story Channel, and every trauma-chic brand manager clung to.

They did not report her story. They curated it.
They did not document the facts. They styled the myth.

What I saw was production.
And what the world applauded was not truth.
It was all marketing.

📝 Beat 2 ~ Violet's Tales from the Margin – Entry #1: "The One We Don't Name."

They do not say her name much anymore.

Not the one that was hers, just the one that made headlines. Just the myth. The mask. The murder.

But I remember her name. The one she whispered when she could not take it anymore. The one she signed on the back of a pharmacy receipt. The one she carved into the side of a Styrofoam cup in the ER.

They erased her so they could remake her.

And now, even the ones who claim to care… only care if it comes with a brand deal.

I sit in the back of this courtroom watching people argue over which tragedy is most profitable and I cannot stop thinking about the girl who just wanted out.

Not of the chair.

Out of the story.

The real one. The ugly one. The one that does not get ratings.

But the real tragedy?

They keep calling her a liar. And they are not entirely wrong.

Because trauma makes storytellers of us all.

But not everyone who survives is ready to tell the truth.

Some of us are still remembering it.

- Violet

Beat 3 ~ My Feather Fell Here

By - Fancy Macelli

"The last person who got in my way is dead."
-Gypsy Rose Blanchard

That is what she whispered into the phone. Cold. Flat. Deliberate.

I did not scream. I did not cry. I sat in silence.

Then I dialed Krusty Blanchard, her stepmother, the same woman I had been working with for over a year on a scripted series called *By Proxy*.

When she answered, I said the only thing I could:
"Your daughter just threatened my life."

That was the moment it all shifted. That was the moment I stopped seeing Gypsy Rose as a victim and started seeing her as what she truly was, someone who could not survive without the script.

That whisper was not a cry for help.
It was a warning.

Gypsy does not handle rejection. She does not reflect when confronted. She retaliates.

In February 224, not long after her release, she publicly called me tyrannical. Cast me as the new Dee Dee. Why? Because I dared to say "no."

She has done this before. To friends. Family. Anyone who stops clapping.

But this time, she was not just spinning the narrative, she was controlling it with the rage of someone who thought she would never be challenged again.

Maybe it was not really about me. Maybe it was about the full interrogation I released, unedited, unscripted. The one where the mask slipped. Where the coldness crept through.

Krusty told a YouTuber, they were not mad about Nick's 16-hour interrogation being public. Just Gypsy's.

Let that sink in.

They were fine exposing the vulnerable, autistic man.
But Gypsy? She had a brand to protect.

And when that protection cracked?
The death threats started.
The smear campaigns followed.
And the silence from her inner circle spoke volumes.

I have seen enough to know one thing:
This was not about survival.
This was about control.

Act 1, Scene 57: Between the Bones – The Cost of Knowing

SECTION HEADER: Forensic Suite
FILED BY: Fancy Macelli & Amy Mackey
FILED UNDER: The Pain of the Truth- Truthful Malfeasance
REALM: Allegorical

Some stories do not dissolve in the light.
They calcify.
They harden beneath the surface until they are sharp enough to cut.

For years, we thought evidence would save this case.
That truth would fracture the myth.
That facts would shield us from the fallout.

We were wrong.

What we uncovered did not just shift our view of Gypsy.
It altered how we move in the world.
How we speak.
How we trust.

Because concern was not met with thanks.
It was met with knives.

People do not want the truth.
They want the performance they paid for.

Kristy did not just protect the lie.
She cast it.

Melissa did not just echo the narrative.
She stylized it.

Mike did not just defend Gypsy.
He reframed Dee Dee's murder as a triumph.

The media did not forget to ask questions.
They chose not to.

These were not passive participants. They were architects.
They painted over red flags in high gloss sympathy.
And when you ask why nobody stopped the play?
It is because they all had tickets to the premiere.

🫀 Act 1, Scene 60: The Anatomy of an Alibi

SECTION HEADER: Memory vs. Myth
FILED BY: Fancy Macelli & Amy Mackey
FILED UNDER: Narrative Self Enhancement- Role Reinforcement
REALM: Forensic

There is a difference between memory and myth.
Between survival and stagecraft.

Psychologists call it *narrative self-enhancement*:
The rewiring of memory to preserve self-image.

Sociologists call it *role reinforcement*:
When you internalize the performance, because the applause feels safer than the truth.

In performance psychology, it is *the paradox of the witness*:
When the audience becomes complicit, not because they believe,
but because they want to.

That is where we were.

Caught between the bones of the facts and the carcass of the lie.

This was not just a girl running from abuse.
This was a machine.
And that machine had gears made of trauma tropes and gears greased with pity.

Gypsy did not bury her mother alone.
She buried the evidence with a crowd of cheerleaders holding shovels and contracts.

Act 1, Scene 58: Fancy's Final Caw

SECTION HEADER: Personal Reflections
FILED BY: Fancy Macelli
FILED UNDER: Accountability Escaping- Wheelchair Misrepresentation
REALM: Allegorical

"The story they sold you wasn't her life; it was her audition tape."

We were not watching a survivor come forward.
We were watching a character be born.

She did not escape abuse.
She escaped accountability.

The wheelchair was not her prison.
It was her spotlight.

And from the very first line,
she knew exactly who her audience was.

Act 1, Scene 59: The Dormouse's Whisper

SECTION HEADER: Court of Painted Roses Intermission
FILED BY: The Dormouse
FILED UNDER: What No One Wanted to Hear- Court of Painted Roses
REALM: Allegorical

What No One Wanted to Hear

"The things that mattered most were the things no one dared to say out loud."
– The Dormouse, Wonderland Archives

In The Court of Painted Roses, no one asked for the truth.
They asked for comfort.
For drama.
For villains and victims with easy answers and Instagram filters.

And when the evidence whispered that, just maybe, things weren't so simple?
The world rolled over and went back to sleep.

Because questioning the myth meant questioning themselves.

To do that, they would have to admit:
1. That a girl in a wheelchair can still be dangerous.
2. That trauma branding is not the same as testimony.
3. That Usurper Queen tears were not truth, they were tactics.
4. That The Mourning Orchid was not a monster. She was a mother.

But the world did not want that story.
So, they dreamt a garish one.
And buried her again.

This time under likes, followers, and Voices of the Vine Broadcast deals.

Act 1 Scene 60: Tea & Testimony: Broadcast 4 – "Checkmate in Progress"

Host: Miss Petunia Verity Cawington

Beat 1 ~ Ledger Tag: [Opening Move – Trial-as-Performance Begins]

[Feather static. A record hums faintly in the background.]

"This is Miss Petunia Cawington, your gossamer witness from the hedgerows of Wonderland, and welcome back to *Tea & Testimony*, where the petals don't just whisper, darling… they prosecute."

"Tonight's whisper? The Queen is dead. The Hatter's circling. And the Peony? Oh, she is blooming with blades."

"We've got players pretending they're pawns, and pawns pretending they don't know their fingerprints are all over the script."

"So, sip something sharp, love. Because this is not a fairytale.
It is a dress rehearsal."

♟ Beat 2 ~ Opening Move – Trial-as-Performance Begins

She did not stumble into the spotlight.
She stepped into it.

Polished.
Poised.
Prepared.

She was not a survivor.
She was a story.

Crafted.
Styled.
Sold.

The truth did not fail her.
It just did not make the cut.

She wore innocence like a costume.
The cameras loved it.
The headlines needed it.

And the public?
They never asked for a second take.

She did not just reframe her life.
She recasts the roles:

- The Mourning Orchid became the villain.
- Silas became the henchman.
- And Gypmydia? She became The Garden's sympathy sweetheart.

The only thing more tragic than the crime...
was how many people applauded the performance.

♟ Beat 3 ~ The Final Move Was not Hers

Krusty curated the survivor arc.
Arun Ramey Scamfield- Esqliar legalized the myth.
Ophidia Serpantina Vexrot syndicated the story.
And the media turned from watchdogs to understudies.

Gypmydia made the first move.
But the final choreography?
That belonged to everyone else who wanted a seat at the table.

They did not tell a story.
They conducted a dress rehearsal on a chessboard where each pawn thought itself free.

In Wonderland,
you do not question the Queen's moves.
You cheer for the coronation.
Even if you are next to be sacrificed.

End of Act 1

♥ The Queen is dead. The players are seated. The performance begins. 🕰

Allegorical Interlude

Act 1, Scene 61: When the Crows Loosen Their Ties

Filed under: Procedural Parody and Satirical Interruptions

There are moments in a case, especially one as maddeningly absurd as this
when the only way to keep speaking the truth…
is to laugh before you scream.

So, from time to time, you will notice the lights flicker.
The feathered court fills with chaos.
And the witnesses may look a little more like metaphors than people.

That is not an accident.

These are our sister segments.
Filed from Wonderland.
Archived by the Crows.
And hosted by a rotating ensemble of theatrical absurdity, forensic satire, and narrative exorcism.

This is where the masks fall off.
Not because they were ripped away…
But because they were so obvious, we had to laugh just to get through it.

You have seen the trial.
Now, let us show you the performance.

 Feather Break: Where Reality Gets a Little Loud

Filed Between the Feathers – Sister Realm Interventions Begin Here

Before we move forward, a small note from the Garden Wire Archives.

You have just spent the last several pages tracing lies through timelines,
dissecting narratives with forensic precision,
and wading through the grief-soaked truth of a mother no one mourned correctly.

It is heavy.
It should be.

But every truth-teller needs a breather.
Even the crows.

So, allow us, just for a moment, to shift the lens.
To change the tempo.
To let the absurdity speak in its own dialect.

From time to time in this book, you will encounter segments filed from our sister realms,
Wonderland, the Garden, the Ledger, and more.

These are stylized, allegorical interludes where the witnesses may be metaphors,
the lawyers may be parodies,
and the court is less about jurisprudence...
and more about just reckoning.

They are not breaks from the truth.
They are truth told sideways,
through satire, surrealism, and theatrical chaos.

So, consider this your official gavel slam:

The trial is in recess.
The theater is in session.
And the Court of The Painted Roses is about to come unhinged.

⚖️ Act 1, Scene 62: Witness Carousel

Filed under: Testimonies, Tiaras, and Truth Rewritten in Crayon

---

🎀 WITNESS #1: GYPMYDIA'S NARRATIVE

(Enter a pastel fairytale creature wrapped in a sympathy cloak and branded hashtags.)

ABSINTHE ROSEMARY HIGHTOPP
State your name for the record.

GYPMYDIA'S NARRATIVE
I'm the brave butterfly, the porcelain phoenix. The face that launched a thousand GiveMeMoney Funds.

ABSINTHE ROSEMARY HIGHTOPP
Is it true you've told multiple versions of key events depending on the platform?

GYPMYDIA'S NARRATIVE *(fluttering)*
I was processing… through algorithms.

♿ WITNESS #2: THE WHEELCHAIR

(It's rolled in like a sacred relic. Decorated with pity stickers and sponsorship logos.)

PROFESSOR BUTTERELLA SNORTLEBOTTUM
This chair gave her comfort! And content!

ABSINTHE ROSEMARY HIGHTOPP
But she walked when unobserved. So, was it mobility or marketing?

HEXIE SERENITY LARUE *(hands raised, eyes closed)*
The Spirit of Dee Dee says, "She needed it, but she needed the attention more."

TRANSCRIPT EXCERPT

Transcript Excerpt 002 — "Wheels of Deception"

Filed: Witness — The Wheelchair

Q&A

TISIPHONE LYSANDRA CHRYSALIS: Were you medically necessary?

THE WHEELCHAIR: Depends on your definition of necessity. I was a tool that became a prop when she no longer wanted to be sick. It's more about the optics.

TISIPHONE LYSANDRA CHRYSALIS: Optics?

THE WHEELCHAIR: Sympathy. Sponsorships. The Guild of Fairy Godmothers parades, and her clients didn't mind, in fact they quite enjoyed it.

TISIPHONE LYSANDRA CHRYSALIS: Did the defendant ever rise from you unassisted?

THE WHEELCHAIR: Frequently. But not when the cameras were rolling.

TISIPHONE LYSANDRA CHRYSALIS: Were you ever part of a lie?

THE WHEELCHAIR: I was the chariot for the lies

TISIPHONE LYSANDRA CHRYSALIS: And the public never questioned you?

THE WHEELCHAIR: They didn't want to. I made the photos sadder.

TISIPHONE LYSANDRA CHRYSALIS: Are you still in use? Are you still in use?

THE WHEELCHAIR: Only in flashbacks but I wait patiently for her inevitable return.

IN THE COURTROOM OF THE PAINTED ROSES
CASE NO. WND-LIE-0113-CR-OP1
Transcript Excerpt 002 — "Wheels of Deception"
Filed: Witness — The Wheelchair

💊 WITNESS #3: THE PILL BOTTLE
(A comically large prescription bottle takes the stand, its cap cracked, label suspiciously "misplaced.")

ABSINTHE ROSEMARY HIGHTOPP
And where were *you* kept?

PILL BOTTLE
That depends. On the story she's telling today.

VONDA LYNNE HEARSAY-DE LUCA
OBJECTION! That bottle is clearly biased and no longer FDA approved.

ABSINTHE ROSEMARY HIGHTOPP
Tell that to the crime scene log.

TRANSCRIPT EXCERPT

Transcript Excerpt 006 — "Prescription for a Plot"

Filed: Witness — The Pill Bottle

Q&A

ABSINTHE ROSEMARY HIGHTOPP: Where were you kept?

THE PILL BOTTLE: Well that's a bit tricky. Sometimes in her purse. Once... I was traded for a unicorn but it turned out to be just a horse with a birthday hat strapped to its head.

ABSINTHE ROSEMARY HIGHTOPPS: Were you locked up?

THE PILL BOTTLE: Allegedly.

ABSINTHE ROSEMARY HIGHTOPP: Did the defendant know your contents?

THE PILL BOTTLE: She memorized me. She curated me.

ABSINTHE ROSEMARY HIGHTOPPS: Were you ever stolen?

THE PILL BOTTLE: I was borrowed... with intent.

ABSINTHE ROSEMARY HIGHTOPP: Were you part of the murder plan?

THE PILL BOTTLE: I was the tool. But I wasn't the hand

ABSINTHE ROSEMARY HIGHTOPP: Final question, Are you still active?

THE PILL BOTTLE: More than you would think but not as much as needed.

IN THE COURTROOM OF THE PAINTED ROSES
CASE NO. WND-LIE-0113-CR-OP1
Transcript Excerpt 002 — "Wheels of Deception"
Filed: Witness — The Wheelchair

👑 WITNESS #4: PRINCESS GYPMYDIA

(A sequined chaos avatar of Gypsy enters, flanked by Instagram filters and conflicting diagnoses.)

PRINCESS GYPMYDIA VERLAIN MARIS CROWLEY
I was helpless. Except when I wasn't. But also, very helpless.

ABSINTHE ROSEMARY HIGHTOPP

Let's discuss the 2015 Facebook messages. Planning a murder isn't helplessness.

PRINCESS GYPMYDIA VERLAIN MARIS CROWLEY
That was a *cry for help*. With emojis.

TRANSCRIPT EXCERPT

Transcript Excerpt 004 — "Timeline Tampering with Royal Permission"

Filed: Witness — Princess Gypmydia Verlaine Maris Crowley

Q&A

BALIFF CLOVIS BRICKHOUSE: Princess Gypmydia, do you swear to tell the truth?

MEDICAL FILE: Exhibit Z. Classified for years. Exhumed by FOPIA (Freedom of Petal Information Act).

GYPMYDIA VERLAINE MARIS CROWLEY: I do... interpretively.

ABSINTHE ROSEMARY HIGHTOPP: How many times have you recounted your escape story?

GYPMYDIA VERLAINE MARIS CROWLEY: Publicly? Six. Privately? Twelve. Cosmically? Infinity.

ABSINTHE ROSEMARY HIGHTOPP: Are any of those versions consistent?

GYPMYDIA VERLAINE MARIS CROWLEY: My tone is consistent. And that's what matters.

ABSINTHE ROSEMARY HIGHTOPP: Did you ever lie to law enforcement?

GYPMYDIA VERLAINE MARIS CROWLEY: No. I performed selectively.

ABSINTHE ROSEMARY HIGHTOPP: Can you confirm the planning of your mother's beheading?

GYPMYDIA VERLAINE MARIS CROWLEY: It was much more brutal than I had written in the drafts. But they were more of suggestion box than a pilot.

ABSINTHE ROSEMARY HIGHTOPP: And you admit to recruiting the co-defendant.

GYPMYDIA VERLAINE MARIS CROWLEY: And you admit to recruiting the co-defendant?

ABSINTHE ROSEMARY HIGHTOPP: Are you aware this is not a screenplay?

GYPMYDIA VERLAINE MARIS CROWLEY: I lost my notes. But if you say so I guess you that's true? But it sure felt like a fairytale.

IN THE COURTROOM OF THE PAINTED ROSES
CASE NO. WND-LIE-0113-CR-OP1
Transcript Excerpt 004 — "Timeline Tampering with Royal Permission"
Filed: Witness — Princess Gypmydia Verlaine Maris Crowley

📁 WITNESS #5 CORDELIA'S MEDICAL FILE

(Petunia solemnly enters. Violet sets down a sealed red folder. A hush falls.)

ABSINTHE ROSEMARY HIGHTOPP
And you, were you ever examined before the trial?

MEDICAL FILE *(quietly, pages fluttering)*
No. I was sealed. Then blamed.

HEXIE SERENITY LARUE *(whispering)*
The spirits speak now. "You chose the myth over the medical chart."

TRANSCRIPT EXCERPT
Transcript Excerpt 007 — "Sealed and Silenced"

Filed: Witness — Cordelia's Medical File

Q&A

ABSINTHE ROSEMARY HIGHTOPP: State your designation for the record.

MEDICAL FILE: Exhibit Z. Classified for years. Exhumed by FOIA.

ABSINTHE ROSEMARY HIGHTOPP: Were you reviewed prior to the public trial?

MEDICAL FILE: No. I was ignored. Narrative came first.

ABSINTHE ROSEMARY HIGHTOPP: Were there diagnoses confirmed within you?

MEDICAL FILE: Yes. Multiple. Rare disorders, genetic flags, documented testing.

ABSINTHE ROSEMARY HIGHTOPP: Were any of these raised in court?

MEDICAL FILE: Not in full. Not in context. Not while she was alive.

ABSINTHE ROSEMARY HIGHTOPP: Did the prosecution examine you?

MEDICAL FILE: Not thoroughly. They preferred reenactments.

ABSINTHE ROSEMARY HIGHTOPP: And what about the media?

MEDICAL FILE: They chose fairy tales over forensics.

SISTER RAVENA SAGE: The spirit speaks. "I told the truth in ink; You buried me in hashtags."

JUDGE FIDELLA WRATH: That's it. I'm closing this dimension.

IN THE COURTROOM OF THE PAINTED ROSES
CASE NO. WND-LIE-0113-CR-OP1
Transcript Excerpt 007 — "Sealed and Silenced"
Filed: Witness — Cordelia's Medical File

⚠️ The Gavel Shatters

Filed under: Courtroom Collapse and Summoning the Unhinged

[Suddenly: Honking. Screaming. A tiny, glitter-stained clown car barrels through the courtroom doors, fishtailing across the tile, knocking over the "In Memoriam: Truth" banner and nearly demolishing the jury box.]

JUDGE FIDELLA ETERNITY WRATH *(ducking)*
Sweet flaming jurisprudence! Who authorized this??

BRIETTA SLANDERELLA GASLIETTE VON OBJECTIONEE *(emerging from the clown car in a burst of glitter and Red Bull)*
We arrive as defenders of narrative integrity and digital delusion!

[From the car's side door tumble the flunkies like a satire grenade.]

- Butterella throws flashcards marked "Feelings = Facts"
- Vonda recites Facebook group slogans like war chants
- Lurletta rips off her wig, revealing a foil tiara, and screams:
  "I CURSE THEE, PROSECUTION! May your FOIA requests be lost in bureaucracy!"

HEXIE SERENITY LARUE *(swaying, arms raised)*
Silence! I'm receiving a transmission from the realm of regrets!

[She pulls out a crystal goblet and starts pouring essential oils onto the legal briefs. The lights flicker. A feather bursts into flame.]

JUDGE FIDELLA ETERNITY WRATH *(ripping off her robe, climbing onto her bench)*
I HAVE HAD IT WITH YOUR DELUSIONAL DISCOURSE CLOWNS!
THIS IS A COURTROOM, NOT A CRYPTID CONVENTION!

[She hurls her gavel, which ricochets off Hobart's binder and embeds itself in the "In Evidence We Trust" plaque.]

ABSINTHE ROSEMARY HIGHTOPP *(quietly collecting her files)*
When you're done summoning spirits and setting precedent by meme, I'll be over here documenting the collapse.

PETUNIA VERITY CAWINGTON *(from the gallery, dryly)*
And I thought Wonderland was absurd.

Court adjourned. No ruling. No closure. Just carnage.

🖼️ *Petal #1 – "Defense Arrives with the Grace of a Shrieking Piñata"*

Illustration: Defense flunkies crash into the courtroom in pink glitter car mid-confetti burst. One clown is splayed across the floor. Hobart is mid-scream. The jury recoils behind a smoke cloud of absurdity.
"Flaming tie. Confetti trauma. Vehicular narrative collapse.

This was the moment the record stopped pretending to be sane." – Violet Darkly

📒 **Ledger Tag:** EXH-A: Vehicular Entrance, Questionable Intent

🖼️ Petal #2 – "Princess Gypmydia Takes the Stand"

Illustration Summary:
The courtroom has transformed into a media circus. PRINCESS GYPMYDIA, cloaked in a glittering powder-blue power suit and rhinestone tiara, sits center stage at the witness stand. Her glasses reflect her ring light, which is mounted beside a comically large "Teleprompter" box. In front of her, a glowing red button, a camera, and a perfectly positioned pie (?) suggest both satire and sabotage. Behind her, dozens of stoics, identically dressed men stare on, frozen mid-bewitchment. Someone in a party hat is levitating. Her smirk is algorithm-approved.

📌 **Caption (Violet's Ledger Voice):**
*"The witness did not swear on a Bible,
she swore on her follower count."
She gave her testimony in takes. Her pauses were deliberate, her lighting pre-set.
When asked what was true, she smiled and adjusted her crown. *
This was not perjury. It was promo.

📁 **Ledger Tag:**
EXH-C: Witness Statement, Monetized

🖼️ Petal #3 – "Hexie LaRue Summons the Spirit"

Illustration Summary:
Sister Hexie Serenity LaRue rises above the bench in a swirl of glowing energy and floating paperwork. Her hands burn with mystical light, one of which is crowned with a crow. The gallery is stunned. A golden orb of narrative confusion spins below her. Smoke. Panic. Clerks whisper prayers.

♣ Caption (Violet's Ledger Voice):

*"She did not file a motion.
She opened a portal."*

The paper rose. The room trembled.
Somewhere between Exhibit A and the afterlife,
Hexie LaRue demanded testimony…
from the dead.

📒 Ledger Tag:

EXH–SE: Seance, Improperly Submitted but Spiritually Overruled

🖼️ Petal #4 – "The Pill Bottle Testifies"

Illustration Summary:
A massive cartoon-style pill bottle sits at the witness stand, weeping uncontrollably. Its label is partially peeled, its childproof cap askew like a bonnet of regret. Crumpled documents marked *Exhibit RX* scatter at its base. To its left, a flunky fans it with a prescription pad. To the right, another lights sage and softly chants, "You were just doing your job." One juror appears to be Googling drug interactions under the desk.

📌 **Caption (Violet's Ledger Voice):**

"It never wanted to be part of the murder."

It just wanted to manage symptoms.
Maybe ease some pain.
Not be held responsible for
an entire genre of YouTube true crime commentary.

The bottle testified bravely.
Between sobs, it confessed its contents.
Between flunkies, it demanded an emotional support gurney.

Someone tried to redact its label.
Someone else offered it a podcast deal.

📒 **Ledger Tag:**

EXH-RX: Side Effects May Include Homicidal Tendencies, TikTok Fame, and Weaponized Sympathy

🖼️ Petal #5 – "Brietta Objects to Herself"

Illustration Summary:

Brietta, appearing in mirrored duplication, stands mid-scream in front of an enormous, cracked vanity mirror etched with courtroom filigree. She wields two microphones like dual pistols. Her reflection is screaming back, equally convinced of her own objection. High heels planted in scattered court documents. The floor is stained pink with legal glitter. Her blazer reads: "OBJECTIONISTA IN CHIEF."

📌 **Caption (Violet's Ledger Voice):**
"She stood before the mirror and saw only injustice.
Then she realized she was the injustice.
So, she objected."
Exhibit boxes were harmed.
Her arguments were written in cursive eyeliner.
At some point, she served herself a subpoena and burst into applause.

📁 **Ledger Tag:**
EXH-BR: Defense Motion, Emotionally Unstable

🖼️ Petal #6 – "The Gavel Goes Rogue"

Illustration Summary (for the book):

In a crescendo of courtroom chaos, JUDGE FIDELLA ETERNITY WRATH is captured mid-meltdown, hurling a flaming gavel across the bench with the precision of divine retribution and the grace of someone fully done. The gavel arcs through a projection screen displaying the Hulu logo, shattering both narrative and decorum. Legal documents swirl like confetti in its wake. One defense flunky shields themselves with a foam-core vision board. The Hatter, seated at the prosecution table, watches silently with her pen lifted mid-sentence. Violet, just visible in the corner, sketches without flinching, her eyes reflecting the fire. A lone crow flies overhead with a post-it in its beak that reads: "Exhibit Z."

🔖 **Caption (Violet's Ledger Voice):**

*"She meant to bang it.
She launched it."*

The gavel flew like justice itself had given up.
It took out a Hulu deal, a motivational poster, and Hobart's third wig.

Somewhere between the objection to logic
and the seance for sympathy,
the judge decided narrative was now a contact sport.

📒 **Ledger Tag:**

EXH-FW: Fidella Wrath – Full Volume

🖼️ Petal #7 – "The Wheelchair Takes the Stand"

Illustration Summary (for the book):
Spotlights glitter across the polished frame of a pastel-pink wheelchair, centered like royalty at the witness stand. Satin bows decorate its handles. A tiny microphone is clipped delicately to one armrest. Behind a roped-off velvet barrier, two defense flunkies crouch reverently one gently misting the wheels with rosewater, the other reading its Miranda rights in a hushed whisper. The gallery watches in stunned silence. One juror clutches a tissue. Another clutches pearls. THE HATTER positioned off to the side, calmly holds up a blown-up photo of the defendant walking through a hotel lobby in flip-flops. Above the courtroom, a holographic banner sparkles: *"EXHIBIT WC – HANDLE WITH NARRATIVE."*

📌 **Caption (Violet's Ledger Voice):**

*"She said it was her prison.
But it was also her platform.
And today, it was her star witness."*

The wheelchair did not testify.
It posed.

The gallery gasped.
The flunkies wept.
And the truth quietly rolled out the back door.

📒 **Ledger Tag:**

EXH-WC: Mobility Exhibit, Photogenic but Problematic

🖼️ Petal #3 – "The Trial Breaks Down"

Illustration Summary (for the book):

All decorum has combusted. The courtroom dissolves into a full-on melee. Clown-suited flunkies are mid-slap fight, wigs and prescription pills raining from above. A defense consultant is caught between two flying binders and a wig to the face. Behind them, a pink wheelchair rolls unattended, and the gallery is frozen in meme-worthy horror. Crows dive bomb through fluorescent lights as one lone nameplate on the bench reads: *"Reserved for Sympathy."* Violet's pen is visible in the corner, sketching at record speed, either documenting or defending herself with line work.

📌 **Caption (Violet's Ledger Voice):**

"And just like that, the trial broke.

*Not in verdict,
but in vibe.*"

The wigs revolted.
The crows descended.
The court reporter stood up and walked out muttering,
'I didn't go to stenography school for this.'

Nobody remembers who threw the first punch.
But everyone remembers who caught the gavel midair.

📒 **Ledger Tag:** EXH-FU: Final Unraveling — Emotional Integrity Compromised

🖼️ Petal #9 – "The Last Witness Falls"

A Three-Part Resolution Scene in Violet's Ledger

🎭 Scene One: Hexie LaRue Collapses

Sister Hexie LaRue stands center courtroom, arms raised, mid-channeling the ghost of Dee Dee. Light swirls around her papers, petals, and medical charts spinning like orbiting moons. But then her eyes roll back, and she collapses theatrically backward into a pile of glowing case files. The flunkies gasp. A crow faints midair.

"She went too deep.
The truth screamed back.
And her bones couldn't carry the contradiction."

Ledger Tag:
EXH-SE.2: Collapse of Clairvoyance – Spiritually Overruled

♿ Scene Two: The Wheelchair Rolls Out

Amid the stunned silence, the pastel wheelchair, no longer adorned or flanked by flunkies, begins to roll away on its own. No one touches it. The room parts. It exits center aisle under a single flickering spotlight. A child's music box version of *"Hallelujah"* plays faintly. Everyone watches it go.

Caption:

*"She called it a prison.
But when the lies cracked,
it rolled itself out."*

Ledger Tag:
EXH-WC.2: Voluntary Exit – Narrative Unseated

✏️ Scene Three: Violet Slams the Ledger

Violet stands atop the jury box, arms shaking. Her expression is unreadable. Her ledger is open wide until, with a sudden snap, she slams it shut. A visible ripple moves across the courtroom: wigs freeze midair, confetti halts, even time catches its breath. All eyes on her.

Caption:

*"She did not argue.
She did not plead.

She simply closed the book.
And the room obeyed." *

Ledger Tag:
EXH-VF: Final Filing – Narrative Sealed by Witness Archivist

🌿 Petal #1 The Queen is Dead

Filed under: Narrative Collapse – Postmortem Mythology

THE QUEEN IS DEAD.
The story she built wore a crown.
But it never wore the truth.

📜 **Eulogy (Petunia or Garden Voice):**

She was never a monarch.
But we called her one because it was easier than naming what she really was.

We crowned her in pity.
We wrapped her in satin lies.
We let her roll through our sympathy unchecked.

And when the truth crawled out with autopsy records, court transcripts, and forgotten diagnoses clinging to its ankles, we looked away.

We let her rewrite a murder into a memoir.
Let her wear her victimhood like velvet.
Let her bury the woman she called "mother" not once, but twice.

First in blood.
Then in branding.

And now, at last,
the throne is empty.
The curtain is ash.
And the crown?
It is cracked, cheap, and no longer fits the facts.

This is not an elegy; it is a reckoning.

Because the Queen is dead.
And we're the ones who handed her the scepter.

Act 1, Scene 63: Broadcast 5: Hold My Lipstick

SECTION HEADER: Garden Broadcast – Cross-Examination Begins
FILED BY: Miss Petunia Verity Cawington
FILED UNDER: Broadcast Analysis – Sympathy Optics – Trial Spectacle
REALM: Allegorical

PETUNIA VERITY CAWINGTON:

Oh, my sweet violets, we must pause right here. Not to mourn, but to replant the truth.

They call it a "ruse," but ruses do not sprout from soil this dense with contradiction. By the time our porcelain petal Gypmydia confessed to cracking, the garden gates had already rusted off the hinges.

The Mourning Orchid was not crafting surgeries in secret. She was navigating storms, both genetic and generational, with a child who had already begun bartering in fantasy and betrayal.

Six springs before the murder, our Gypmydia was already dancing through the hedges in full stride. Walking. Whispering. Wandering. And let me tell you something about our dear Lance of the Decaying Vine, he was no rescuer. He was a rotten root, and Gypmydia chased his scent like nightshade in heat.

She did not run to escape. She ran to perform.
To test the script.
To see if the garden would believe her when she rewrote her roots.

And her kinfolk?
The Shadow King and Krusty of the Velvet Veil?
They did not prune the weeds.
They watered them.

 Whisper from the Weeds

Filed by the Thorn-Watchers, Keepers of the Overgrowth

Whispered Ledger Entry

We saw her long before the roses bloomed.
She was already bending the stalk. Already rehearsing her plea.

She called the garden a prison but walked its length without chains.
She wore the chair when it bought sympathy.
She ditched it when the woodsman came calling.

And what was her "final straw"?
Not a blade.
Not a scream.
Just a whisper from the wind that her mother knew the truth and would not let her own daughter twist it.

She did not slay the lie.
She feared losing authorship.

That is the secret rustling through the weeds:
When Gypmydia realized she could no longer control the story, she uprooted the gardener.

Not for freedom.
For narrative dominance.

🩸 The weeds remember.
We saw the script before the curtain rose.

 Act 1, Scene 64: Closing Statement by Absinthe Rosemary Hightopp

SECTION HEADER: *The High Gallery of the Court of Painted Roses*
FILED BY: Miss Absinthe Rosemary Hightopp
FILED UNDER: Broadcast Analysis - Sympathy Optics - Trial Spectacle
REALM: Allegorical

Satirical Truth-Telling with a Gavel in One Hand and a Garden Shear in the Other

Beat 1 ~ Absinthe's Rebuttal

Well now, isn't that a tangled little trellis of revisionist memory?

We have sat through enough southern church funerals and county fair talent shows to know a rehearsed monologue when we hear one, and this whole "final straw" performance from Miss Gypmydia? It doesn't hold up under the stage lights.

One minute she is the child who could not walk.
Next minute she is dodging curfews in motel rooms, BB gun in one hand and Happily Never After Studios DVD in the other.
She says she feared for her life, yet she was plotting in glitter pens and online chatrooms like a tween with a vendetta and a broadband connection.

And let's talk about that diagnosis, oh yes, the one quietly clipped out of the televised script like an unsightly dandelion at a garden party.

They did not bury it. They removed it completely.

Why?

Because a genetic disorder with cognitive impact does not sell as cleanly as a fairytale captivity tale.
Because the moment you admit she had delays, real, medical, documentable delays, then Mama wasn't inventing a thing.
She was managing a truth the rest of them could not market.

And the rest of that family?

The Shadow King strumming guitars of selective memory.
The Seamstress painting over the bloodstains with Hulu contracts and lemon-scented sympathy.

They were not victims of a lie.
They were co-producers.

So no, honey. This was not a rescue.
It was a rewrite.

And here in the Garden's Court of Public Opinion, we do not buy silence disguised as innocence.

🪶 Beat 2 ~ The Public's Verdict Delivered:

"This wasn't a girl trapped in a tale.
This was a narrator who killed off the author."

Now put that in your memoir and skip the audiobook this time we prefer the unabridged version.

🌸 Beat 3 ~ Garden Gavel Moment

🎭 Filed by: Ruby Begonia Cawington, Grand Dame of Truth & Thorny Takedowns
🔔 Category: Civic Awakening & Forensic Reclamation
🎈 Jurisdiction: The Court of Public Opinion & Southern Sass Supreme

🔔 Beat 4 ~ Let the Record Reflect:

If you have made it this far, you ain't just sipping the tea.
You are stirring the whole damn pot.

Now listen here, sweetpea:

Gypsy did not just rewrite her story.
She tore the pages out of her mama's book, scribbled over the margins, and handed the rest of us a coloring sheet labeled "survivor."

But we see the bleed-through.
We see the ghost ink.
We see the genetic deletion she removed.

Act 1, Scene 65~ Tending The Truth

SECTION HEADER: *From the Bench of Bitter Blooms & Better Truths*
FILED BY: The Ledger of the Silent Witnesses
FILED UNDER: Next Steps
REALM: Allegorical

🪶 *"If they won't ask the questions, we'll plant the answers."*

So, here is what you do next, sweetpea:

 Step One:

Keep tending the truth. This book is only the beginning. The weeds may be thick, but our roots run deeper. Follow the full timeline, the unsealed FOIA, and the contradictions they buried every page matters.

 Step Two:

Support awareness efforts because lies get lonely when truth rides shotgun through the French Quarter. Justice has wheels now, and it knows where the bodies are buried. You can find out more at https://justicefordeedeeandnick.com

 Step Three:

Preorder: *The Girl in the Glass Garden* and *Cawing Out the Truth: Part Two.* The next chapters crack open the courtroom curtain, dissect the media's misdirection, and pull the petals off the real public relations plan behind the murder of Clauddinea Pitre Blanchard.

 Step Four:

Ask your local station this:
"Why do they keep giving airtime to Gypsy without ever mentioning the genetic diagnosis she redacted, or the eight conflicting POA forms signed in 2013 with at least two fake birthdates?"
We are not just readers; we are witnesses now.

🪶 *They can edit the tapes. But they cannot edit us.*

 Final Petal:

The story did not unravel because Gypsy escaped.
It unraveled because someone started stitching it back together—with facts, not fan fiction.

So darlin,' press your petals, raise your voice, and let 'em know:

- *Justice blooms where the weeds once whispered.*
- *The Garden has reopened.*
- *And we are pruning lies by the root.*

Act 1, Scene 66: Curtain Drop – Final Reflection

Filed by Fancy Macelli, Truth Archivist, Witness Advocate, and Unapologetic Crow

They will not like this act.

They will say it is cruel.
Too harsh.
Too complicated.
Too unwilling to let a girl in a wheelchair remain a girl in a wheelchair.

But that is the point.

Because she was not just a girl in a wheelchair.
She was not just a victim.
And Dee Dee was not just a monster.

They were people.
With flaws, with pain, with stories that did not fit neatly into hashtags.

And somewhere in the middle of that mess,
a crime happened.
A mother was murdered.
A boy was used.
A nation was lied to.

And we clapped.

But not anymore.

This was the part where the curtain falls.
Where the props get packed away.
Where the real witnesses, those never called to the stand, finally speak.

The wheelchair rolled out.
The gavel broke.
The ledger closed.

And the Queen?

She is dead.

Chapter One: **The Anatomy of a Manufactured Victim**
Filed. Sealed. And ready for cross-examination.

🕵️ Act 1, Scene 67: Choose Your Own Reckoning

Filed Between Chapters – Optional Diversion for the Incurably Curious

Before you turn the page, take a breath.
Then ask yourself:
What story did *you* just believe?

Because this is not just a book.
It is a courtroom.
And you, dear reader, just served on the jury.
So, now is your chance to retrace your steps or double down on the performance.

Choose your next path:

🔍 1. Open Exhibit Z – Re-Examine the Evidence

Go back to Violet's Ledger and read the captions without laughing. We dare you.
  📍 Jump to: **Violet's Ledger – Petals on the Bench**

🤡 2. Follow the Flunkies to TikTok

You have heard the arguments. Now watch the memes. See how sympathy was stylized into content.
  📍 Jump to: **Cra Cra and the Courtroom – Witness Carousel**

🦴 3. Read the Autopsy First This Time

Ignore the performance. Forget the tiara. Go straight to the forensic truth Dee Dee never got.
  📍 Jump to: **Bone Shard Glossary – Myth Maintenance Suite**

♿ 4. *Interview the Wheelchair*

Ask the one witness that never spoke but said everything.
- 📍 Jump to: **Petal #7** – "The Wheelchair Takes the Stand"

👁 5. *Move On Like the Media Did*

Turn the page. Forget the crime. Start fresh with a new case study. Jennifer Pan awaits.
- 📍 Proceed to: **Chapter Two** - The Rebranding of a Corpse

⚠️ Whatever path you choose, remember...Act 1 was only the opening statements. The witnesses you've met, the evidence you've seen, and the verdicts you've formed are all about to be tested. In the next act, the lights get harsher, the transcripts get longer, and the stories you thought you understood start contradicting themselves in real time. This is where the fairy tale frays, and where the record starts talking back.

🎙 *Act 1, Scene 68: Tea & Testimony ~ "Before the Gavel Falls"*

Episode Title:
[Sound: the gentle clink of porcelain, the low hum of a kettle, faint garden ambience.]

RUBY BEGONIA CAWINGTON:
Have you ever noticed how the truth never shows up to the trial on time?

PETUNIA VERITY CAWINGTON:
Mm. That's because it gets stopped at the door for wearing the wrong dress.

RUBY BEGONIA CAWINGTON:
(laughs) And meanwhile, the lie's already inside, waving to the cameras and making friends with the jury.

PETUNIA VERITY CAWINGTON:
Today's case in point what we've been sipping on for the past year. Is a story sold in sequins and sympathy, with the receipts locked in the lady's lavatory.

RUBY BEGONIA CAWINGTON:
They called it "justice." But it was just theater with a corpse offstage.

PETUNIA VERITY CAWINGTON:
And the audience? They clapped. They bought the merch. They posted their unthought pieces. Never mind the parts they didn't see the evidence left out, the timelines that didn't line up, the so-called experts whose credentials were more glitter than gold.

RUBY BEGONIA CAWINGTON:
Which is why we're here, my dear buttercups. To remind you that before the gavel falls, the story has already been written and usually, it's written by the people who stand to gain.

PETUNIA VERITY CAWINGTON:
So, pour yourself something strong. Act 1 is coming to a close, and before we step into Act 2, we're going to walk you through how the myth got made, how the truth got trimmed, and why some of us refuse to let the ending stick, because it failed to land.

Act 1, Scene 69: Letters from the Mourning Orchid

Filed under: *Petal Promises, Withheld Whispers, and the Ledger of Unfinished Goodbyes*
Delivered by Ravenna during the twilight recess of the Court of Public Opinion.

Beat 1 ~ The Mourning Orchid Speaks - Open Ledger Entry 5.6.1

From Dee Dee ~ The Mourning Orchid:

To all who stood in the storm because I could not speak,

They told my story without me.
They cut my name down to a headline, my life to a lesson, my love to a crime.

But you sifted through the lies.
And truth from sealed files
from whispers in court hallways,
from the pages no one wanted read aloud.

You saw me not as the villain they painted,
but as a mother, flawed, human, and
deserving of a defense I never received.

You gave me what the system never did:
A voice.
A chance to stand in the light.
A record that says I was here,
and I mattered.

When the world bought the fairytale,
you tended to the roots of the truth.
When they crowned my KILLER a princess,
you refused to let my ashes be the throne.

So, I leave you with this:
Do not stop.
Do not let them sell another life for ratings.
Do not let another mother be silenced
before the first question is even asked.

You think I am Gone.
I'm in every Thorne
But my story is no longer theirs to profit from
It is yours to protect.

Keep it. Guard it. Tell it.
And know that in every fight
you take on for the silenced,
I am there.

Standing beside you
in a place where truth doesn't bend
to the highest bidder.

Thank you, my Beautiful Garden Friends,

Dee Dee ~ The Mourning Orchid

Beat 2 ~ The Mourning Orchid Speaks – Open Ledger Entry 5.6.2

To Krusty Crowley, From the Memory You Buried Alive

"You called her daughter. Claimed her crown. Wore her name like warpaint.

But I remember the night you rehearsed your rise, while I still lay cooling in the coroner's drawer.

I watched you.

Framing your sainthood through my ash.

I was already dead.

But you needed me more useful than that.

So, you dragged my legacy to the morgue and used my bones to buy yourself a story.

But I am not your prologue, KRUSTY.

I am your ghost.

And I will haunt every script you stole."

Beat 3 ~ The Mourning Orchid Speaks - Open Ledger Entry 5.6.3

Dear Fancy,

I never go to give you a proper hello.
They turned my petals into poison.
They took my love, dressed it in suspicion, and
asked the world to applaud.

But I remember.

I remember your voice on the edge of the storm.
I remember the ledger you kept before there was ink to fill it.
You came looking not for vengeance, but for the roots.
And I owe you the truth of the garden I tried to grow.
They call it the Curse of the Crown now.

But I called it survival.
I called it "just one more night, one more spoonful, one more prescription that might let her sleep."
I called it love.

You see, they let the performance speak before the patient.
They let the narrative bloom without water.
And by the time the cameras rolled, my daughter had forgotten the soil she sprouted from.

They handed her crowns and cameras and captions,
and she learned how to smile through a smear.
But she was not evil.
And I was not a monster.
We were broken, bruised women on opposite ends of a locked door,
both begging someone to come in and just ask the right question.

You did.
You always did.

Even when the wind said stop,
even when they threw salt at your name,
even when you stood alone in a courtroom where silence was currency.

So now, I ask one thing more:
Don't forget me.

Do not let them write me out of my own bloom cycle.
Do not let my death be the seed of a lie.
Let it be the start of truth.
I was her mother.
And I loved her.
Even when she stopped loving me.

In memory and in mourning,
always yours beneath the mulch,
 🌸 *The Mourning Orchid*

Beat 4 ~ The Mourning Orchid Speaks ~ Open Ledger Entry 5.6.4

From the Shade of the Cypress ~ Dee Dee Speaks to Mack & Fancy

My girls...

You showed up for me when the world walked away.

You picked up the pieces they scattered for ratings, and you stitched them back together with truth and thunder. You said my name when it wasn't safe to say it. You spoke up when silence was easier. You told the truth when lies were trending.

And Lord, I watched.

I watched them laugh at you, doubt you, drag your names across the mud like they did mine. I watched you face the smear campaigns, the slander, the death threats, the smirks from people who've never read a damn medical record.

And you never blinked.

You stood your ground in courtrooms that weren't real, and some that were, but it sure as hell mattered. You dug through dumpsters of denial and documentary cuts. You pieced together what even the police didn't bother to learn.

Fancy, you brought the fire.

Mack, you brought the light.

Together? You made a torch that burns through the box they hide me in.

And now you're doing something no one thought possible: you're not just clearing my name you have created a movement for justice.

Dee Dee's Law.

My God. If I had breath left in these lungs, I'd use it to shout your names from every rooftop they claimed I jumped off. You are rewriting what justice looks like for women like me, for mamas who died in the shadow of their child's performance. For victims who didn't wear the right costume. For truth-tellers who couldn't afford a press tour.

You're not just avenging me. You're protecting the next mother who dares to raise her child without applause or apology.

You're giving me something they tried to take, my dignity.

And more than that you're giving yourselves something even more rare:

Peace. Through purpose.

Ladies, keep going. Keep writing. Keep burning the scripts they handed you and carving your own into the record.

They called me a witch. You're showing them I was a warning.

You're not just my voice.
You're my vindication.

I tip my crown you both.

Now go.
Finish what you've started.

We are Gen ✖.
Generation ✖ doesn't just call out the lie,
we drag it into the light and dare it to blink.

We're the last ones who learned to fight
without filters, stand without scripts,
and keep swinging when the crowd fights back.

You didn't just back me
you became the fight itself,
and history won't be able to write me
without writing you.

And take my name all the way to the hill.

God Speed.
Dee Dee, The Mourning Orchid
(Forever your third girl in the foxhole.)

Beat 5 ~ The Mourning Orchid Speaks - Open Ledger Entry 5.6.5

From Dee Dee: Closing to the Court of Public Opinion

Honorable Keepers of the Garden's Law, I lay my petals before you, not as the wilted relic they painted, but as the rooted truth they tried to dig up and discard. The weeds of false witness have climbed my name, their blooms fed by profit and spectacle, but you have seen past their perfume. I stand here not to beg, but to bear witness.

You have heard the lies dressed in lace, the half-truths sold as whole, the stories that profited from my silence. You have walked through the rows of evidence, brushed the dirt from the seeds they buried, and found me here still standing in the soil of fact. Let the record in this realm show: the Mourning Orchid will not be pressed flat in their scrapbook of convenient fables. Let it show that the crown they forged from my absence is already cracking, and that in this Court, truth will flower long after their lies have gone to seed.

I was not given my day in this court when I lived, so I take it now in death, through the voices that refused to let me vanish. Let the record show that my name will not be left in the hands of those who took my life or rewrote it for gain. Let it show that truth outlasts performance, and that the crown they forged from my blood will rust.

And when you render your verdict, remember this was never just my case. It is the case for every silenced victim who still waits for their truth to be called to the stand.

Act 1, Scene 70: Closeout: The Verdict You Didn't Know You Rendered

Every page you've turned in Act 1 has been testimony, some sworn, some spun, all strategically staged. We've walked through planted evidence and manicured myths, heard the case for a princess in peril, and seen the defense for a mother who never got her day in court. You've been handed flowers to hide the grave. You've seen the petals painted, the thorns tucked in.

And here's the uncomfortable truth: verdicts are not handed down by gavels alone. They are shaped in living rooms, on newsfeeds, in hashtags, and in hearts that would rather be comforted than confronted.

Act 1 also ends where it always should have begun and that's with Dee Dee.

She was not perfect, but she was a mother, a daughter, a sister, and a friend whose life mattered. She was not a headline or a diagnosis for someone else's profit. She did not deserve to be reduced to the villain in a stranger's script, stripped of context, and erased from her own story.

Over these scenes, we've torn back the first layer of deceit: the media didn't just report her death they gift-wrapped it, sold it, and cashed the check. Prosecutors and alleged "experts:" didn't just overlook the truth. They abandoned it in plain sight. And those who stood to gain didn't just keep quiet they built careers on the silence. The public was handed a glittered fairytale because the real story was messy, ugly, and dangerous to the people making money off the lie.

Dee Dee deserves better than that. The record deserves better than that. And the people who still care enough to read past the headlines deserve the full truth.

From the start, the media was not a neutral observer, it was an active architect. National outlets packaged the case in pink ribbons and pity, crafting a ready-made narrative of "abused daughter, monstrous mother." One that sold easily to viewers and advertisers. Details that complicated that image conflicting timelines, untested evidence, and court records that contradicted Gypsy's claims were buried or ignored entirely. By the time the first jury was ever seated, the public had already been given its verdict, not from the bench, but from morning talk shows, docudramas, and magazine spreads. In that way, the trial was less about evidence and more about sustaining a marketable myth, one headline at a time.

Dee Dee's Law was born because of betrayal and injustice. It is a line in the sand against killers and their accomplices turning murder into merchandise. No books. No film deals. No glossy interviews that turn the guilty into celebrities while the victim is buried twice once in the ground, and again under a mountain of lies. It is a call to protect victims especially those who can no longer speak for themselves from being exploited in death by those responsible for their annihilation.

Dee Dee's Law would bar convicted murderers and their accomplices from profiting off their crimes through books, films, interviews, or merchandise, and it would extend protections to safeguard the victim's name from defamation disguised as entertainment. It is both a shield for the silenced and a warning to the opportunists: you cannot turn blood into lies and call it a rebrand. Telling "your truth" does in no way equate to a paycheck. How dare you make a living rewriting the truth and defaming your victim. We intend to bring that to an end. Victims should have voices too. To sign Dee Dee's Law, scan the QR code below. We can't wait to see you get involved.

Appendix A – The Index of Permissible Proofs

(Filed under: Narrative Forensics – Source Authentication – Chain of Custody for the Truth)

Note: The following references are presented in **APA 7th edition** style to maintain admissibility in both scholarly review and our own allegorical court.

Academic / Forensic Citations

Hartwig, M., & Bond, C. F. (2011). Statement Analysis and SCAN: Validity and reliability issues. *Law and Human Behavior, 35*(4), 341–355. https://doi.org/10.xxxx/lhb.2011.04

Vrij, A. (2008). *Detecting lies and deceit: Pitfalls and opportunities* (2nd ed.). Wiley.

Ekman, P. (2009). *Telling lies: Clues to deceit in the marketplace, politics, and marriage* (4th ed.). W. W. Norton & Company.

Federal Bureau of Investigation. (n.d.). Statement analysis. *FBI Law Enforcement Bulletin.* https://leb.fbi.gov/

Media / Documentary References

HBO. (2017). *Mommy dead and dearest* [Documentary film]. HBO Documentary Films.

Hulu. (2019). *The act* [Television series]. Hulu Originals.

Memoir

Blanchard, G. R. (2024). *My time to stand.* [Publisher].

News / Press

Bernstein, J. (2015, June 16). Gypsy Rose Blanchard: Inside the twisted murder case. *Springfield News-Leader.* https://www.news-leader.com/

Law Enforcement Records

Springfield Police Department. (2015, June). *Gypsy Rose Blanchard interrogation transcript.* Springfield, MO.

Public Records & FOIA Disclosures

Greene County Court. (2015–2024). *FOIA filings: Police, court, and medical records.* Springfield, MO.

Medical/Legal Records

Steele, [First initial]. (2001–2015). *Patient records for Gypsy Rose Blanchard.* [Hospital/Clinic].
State of Louisiana. (2001). *Power of attorney filing for Clauddine Blanchard.* [Court].
Genetic Diagnostics Lab. (2001). *Chromosome microarray results: 1q21.1 microdeletion.*
Missouri Department of Social Services, Child Protective Services. (2009–2015). *CPS reports and interventions.*

Private Communications

Blanchard, G. R., & Godejohn, N. P. (2015, June). *Text message exchanges.* Springfield Police Department Evidence Unit.

Expert Commentary

Weber, M. (2019). Commentary on the Blanchard case. *MCA Investigations Internal Report.* Interview Conducted by Fancy Macelli

---

Literary Quotations

Carroll, L. (1871). *Through the looking-glass, and what Alice found there.* Macmillan.
Poe, E. A. (1845). *The raven, and other poems.* Wiley and Putnam.

Internal Media Productions

Fancy Macelli Media. (2024). *Gathering of the crows* [Podcast].
Fancy Macelli Media. (2024). *America's sweetheart murderers* [Podcast series].

Appendix B – The Bone Shard Glossary

(Filed under: Forensic Translation – Narrative Dissection – Symbol & Statement Alignment)

These are the **technical and forensic terms** that anchor our analysis the language of evidence, stripped of allegory so it can stand in court.

1. **Narrative Pivot Delay**: The intentional postponement of introducing key narrative shifts to control audience reaction or adapt to new evidence.
2. **Emotional Alibi Construction**: The deliberate shaping of emotional expression to substitute for factual defense in testimony.
3. **Narrative Restitution**: The act of reclaiming or rewriting a narrative to restore perceived ownership or moral high ground.
4. **Body Mapping Revenge**: The symbolic use of harm, markings, or injuries to communicate intent or signature in a crime.
5. **Learned Helplessness**: A psychological state where repeated exposure to inescapable adverse situations conditions the subject to stop attempting escape or defense.
6. **Symbolic Distortion**: The alteration of symbolic or allegorical elements to reframe moral alignment.
7. **Myth Maintenance**: Sustaining a false narrative through repetition, selective sourcing, and audience targeting.
8. **Narrative Self-Enhancement**: Amplifying one's own role in a story for self-promotion or image control.
9. **Emotional Alibi**: Relying on an emotive presentation to discredit contrary facts.
10. **Social Role Enforcement**: The pressure exerted by societal expectations to act in a manner consistent with a pre-assigned identity.
11. **Role Reinforcement**: The repetitive use of behaviors or claims to solidify a chosen public role.
12. **Retcon (Retroactive Continuity)**: A narrative technique in which previously established facts are rewritten or ignored in later versions of a story, usually to benefit the protagonist or fit a new agenda. *(Beat 3 ~ Bone Shard Sidebar: The Origin of the Rebrand*
13. **Memory Laundering**: Altering or re-contextualizing memories to cleanse them of damaging implications.
14. **Fantasy Rehearsal**: Mentally practicing a desired event or outcome before its execution.
15. **Strategic Humiliation**: The targeted use of embarrassment or degradation to gain a psychological or narrative advantage.

🌿 Appendix C – The Garden Vines Glossary

(Filed under: Allegorical Translation – Realm-Specific Lexicon – Symbolism Index)

These are the **realm-bound allegorical terms,** the living vines that run between the roots of the Primal Vein and the petals of the Garden. They are not meant to be read as literal fact, but as the symbolic truth spoken in the Court of Painted Roses.

1. **Cult of the DeLuLus:** Devotees of a rewritten reality; worshippers of the Usurper Queen's version of events.
2. **The Curse of the Crown:** The burden or destructive consequence that follows the assumption of a false or stolen role of power.
3. **The Ledger:** The master record of the Court; contains all testimony, both true and false, and judges them in time.
4. **The Pink Script:** The ceremonial rewrite; a script that replaces inconvenient reality with a pastel, marketable version.
5. **Victimhood Crown™:** The ornamental proof of suffering in the realm of public opinion; can be worn, displayed, or sold.
6. **Weeds of the Garden:** Invasive truth-tellers that push through cracks where lies have trampled the ground.

Appendix D: The Witness Roll – Flesh, Feather & Fabrication

(Real Characters – Act 1 Cast Index)

Aleah Woodmansee: *(Act 1, Beat 6)*
Friend and confidante to Gypsy Rose, receiving texts in which Gypsy disclosed the 1q21.1 deletion and her relationship with Nick Godejohn. A quiet but pivotal witness whose knowledge challenges the later media script.

Amy Mackey: *(Act 1, Prologue Scene 5)*
Co-author and investigative partner. The other half of the Ledger's twin pens, bringing grounded scrutiny and a refusal to let narratives go unchallenged.

Dr. Bernardo Flasterstein: *(Act 1, Beat 6)*
Neurologist who challenged the prevailing medical narrative, his skepticism forming a fracture point in the narrative by suggesting possible MBP.

Casey Anthony: *(Act 1, Beat 6)*
Parallel cultural touchstone for media manipulation and contested motherhood narratives.

Celeste Blanchard: *(Act 1, Beat 6)*
Rod's sister. She was the first to contact Gypsy in prison. The phone call was strange and interesting from a woman Gypsy allegedly had not seen in near a decade.

Claudia Pitre: *(Act 1, Beat 6)*
Dee Dee's older sister. Claudia is who told Gypsy that Dee Dee made her life miserable and they didn't need to even get her body from the morgue further humiliation of Dee Dee. Falsey showed the world that nobody cared because Dee Dee was so horrible even though her family didn't want her.

Clauddine "Dee Dee" Blanchard: *(Act 1, Beat 7)*
Mother of Gypsy Rose, painted by the media as the ultimate villain. In the Ledger, she becomes both victim and contested figure, her memory clouded by the Pink Script.

Detective Stan Hancock: *(Act 1, Beat 10)*
Lead investigator in the case, noted for identifying Gypsy's "past tense slip" as a tell of foreknowledge.

Diane Downs: *(Act 1, Beat 6)*
Historical case example of maternal filicide, used in the Ledger to frame patterns in public sympathy and deception.

Dr. Robert Beckerman: *(Act 1, Beat 6)*
Medical professional appearing in the timeline, illustrating gaps between testimony, diagnoses, and documented care.

Dr. Robert Steele: *(Act 1, Beat 6)*
Gypsy's Primary Care Physician from 2005-2015. Dr. Steele claimed he did not have access to Gypsy's previous medical records despite receiving them one month after she landed in Kansas City.

Erin Caffey: *(Act 1, Beat 6)*
Comparative case underscoring patterns of calculated violence cloaked in victimhood.

Fancy Macelli: *(Act 1, Prologue Scene 5)*
Co-author and forensic narrator of the Ledger. Wields both the paper trail and the allegorical blade, cutting through cultivated myths with precision and dark wit.

Gypsy Rose Blanchard: *(Act 1, Beat 7)*
The Usurper Queen of the real-world trial, accused of murdering her mother. At once a cultural icon and an unreliable narrator of her own history.

Dr. Jean Pierre Le Pichon: *(Act 1, Beat 6)*
Specialist physician discovered the 1q21.1 microdeletion giving Dee Dee the answers she finally needed.

Jennifer Pan: *(Act 1, Beat 6)*
Referenced comparative case, illustrating thematic parallels in manipulation and narrative construction.

Kristy Blanchard: *(Act 1, Beat 7)*
Husband Stealer, Posthumous Defamer and Downright Greedy. Kristy is who largely pushed the false narrative to the press.

Mike Callais: *(Act 1, Beat 6)*
Relative to Rachel Callais, tied to early biographical context in the Ledger's reconstruction. He claims to have helped Dee Dee get the Habitat House despite claiming he had to throw Dee Dee and Gypsy out of their house 2 years prior alleging that Dee Dee was poisoning his elderly mom.

Mike Stanfield: *(Act 1, Beat 6)*
Gypsy Rose's attorney turned brand manager, serving as both her legal shield and her public-stage handler. In the Ledger, his narrative is dissected for contradictions, selective disclosures, and the quiet architecture of a rebrand.

Mike Webber: *(Act 1, Beat 6)*
Tarrant County Texas District Attorney's Office investigator. Expert on medical child abuse.

Nicolette: *(Act 1, Beat 6)*
Gypsy's half-sister. She is 6 months younger than Gypsy. Her mother is Jill, Rod's high school girlfriend. He got her pregnant at 15 and abandoned her and their child.

Nick Godejohn: *(Act 1, Beat 7)*
Gypsy's co-defendant and romantic partner, cast alternately as accomplice and monster depending on the teller.

Rachel Callais: *(Act 1, Beat 6)*
See Mike Callais. Wife of Mike Callais and listed on the 2013 POA with the conflicting birth dates.

Rachel Miller: *(Act 1, Beat 6)*
Family acquaintance in MO. Listed on the 2013 POA with the conflicting birth dates.

Ray Miller: *(Act 1, Beat 6)*
Family acquaintance in MO. Listed on the 2013 POA with the conflicting birth dates.

Rod Blanchard: *(Act 1, Beat 7)*
Gypsy's father, absent for much of her life yet drawn into the media's narrative web. A figure whose silence speaks volumes in court filings and FOIA records.

Appendix E: The Witness Roll – Flesh, Feather & Fabrication

(Allegorical Characters – Act 1 Cast Index)

Absinthe Rosemary Hightopp: *(Act 1, Prologue Scene 5)*
The Prosecutor in the Court of the Painted Roses. A hatter of logic and cross-examination, whose eccentricity hides a surgical precision in cutting apart falsehoods.

Bailiff Clovis Brickhouse: *(Act 1, Beat 4)*
Stone-faced guardian of the allegorical court, ensuring decorum even when truth and lies start to brawl in the aisles.

Brietta Slanderella Gasliette Von Objection: *(Act 1, Scene 7)*
Editor-in-Chief of Pink-Script Publishing and sworn defender of the Usurper Queen. Specializes in rewriting facts until they wear a sympathetic shade of blush.

Captain Gladiola "Glady" Ethereal Storm: *(Act 1, Beat 4)*
A storm-drenched enforcer from the outer gardens, tasked with carrying messages no one wants to hear but everyone needs to know.

Cordelia Crowley – The Mourning Orchid: *(Act 1, Beat 2)*
The Red Queen/Princess figure, cut down before her second bloom. A living emblem of a truth too delicate for the Pink Script to survive.

Court Reporter Sybilla Quill: *(Act 1, Beat 4)*
The silent scribe of allegorical proceedings, recording every metaphor and misstep for posterity's reckoning.

Detective Jasper Ransom Cain: *(Act 1, Beat 4)*
Hound of the hedge-mazes, adept at sniffing out deceit in both the real and allegorical realms.

Garden of Silent Witnesses: *(Act 1, Beat 2)*
The ancient root-keepers beneath the Garden, storing the pulse of unspoken truths until the lies grow too bloated to stand.

Gypmydia Verlaine Maris Crowley – The Usurper Queen: *(Act 1, Beat 2)*
A frail bloom crowned in sympathy and spun into legend by the Cult of the DeLuLus. Her reign is less about ruling than rewriting.

Hobart Gaveldozer Wretched Jr.: *(Act 1, Beat 4)*
A hammer-wielding enforcer of courtroom order, fonder of the gavel's weight than the law's letter.

Hexie Serenity LeRue: *(Act 1, Beat 4)*
Warden of the wilting petals, tending to those crushed in the slow collapse of false narratives.

Judge Fidella Eternity Wrath: *(Act 1, Beat 4)*
The gavel as final word. Her judgments split lies like lightning splits the night, yet even she must weigh the stories' thorns.

Lunetta "Lunk" Skreachington: *(Act 1, Beat 4)*
An eccentric court fixture whose bumbling facade hides a knack for unearthing inconvenient truths.

Marigold Finch Tinch: *(Act 1, Beat 4)*
The Chief Editor of the Garden Wire Newspaper. Bright-plumed but sharp-eyed, she carries whispers between the branches of truth and deceit.

Petunia Verity Cawington: *(Act 1, Beat 4)*
One of the three black-feathered Silent Witness sisters. The curator of truths too bitter for sugar.

Professor Butterella Snortlebottom: *(Act 1, Beat 4)*
Unscholar of improbable facts, whose lectures stitch together fables, files, and the forensic footnotes no one can make heads or tails of.

Ravena Sage: *(Act 1, Beat 4)*
The dusk-voiced keeper of warnings, known for prophesying the collapse of false crowns.

Ruby Begonia Cawington: *(Act 1, Beat 4)*
Silent Witness sister with a knack for plucking the threads of a lie until it unravels in public.

Tangie Amarantha Whiteviel: *(Act 1, Prologue Scene 5)*
The Narrative Archivist. One foot in the Court, one in Wonderland's shadow, ferrying truths from the veil beyond where victims can no longer speak.

The Past Tense: *(Act 1, Scene 11)*
Not a person but a specter, it slips from the tongue of the guilty, revealing what they know before they mean to.

The Weeds: *(Act 1, Beat 2)*
Uninvited chroniclers of the Garden, sprouting wherever truth has been trampled. Persistent, unpretty, and impossible to root out.

Tisiphone Lysandra Chrysalis: *(Act 1, Prologue Scene 5)*
The Co-Counsel in the Court of the Painted Roses, whose silky patience belies a predator's precision.

Violet Darkly Cawington: *(Act 1, Beat 4)*
The darkest plumed of the Silent Witness sisters. Keeps the archive of the things no one else will say aloud.

Vonda Lynn Heanspray: *(Act 1, Beat 4)*
A peacock of the press gallery, spreading rumors like glitter sticking to everything and impossible to sweep away.

Appendix E: The Witness Roll – Flesh, Feather & Fabrication

(Object & Concept Characters – Act 1 Cast Index)

Gypmydia's Narrative: *(Act 1, multiple scenes)*
Not just a story, but a living construct she wears like armor. Flexible when it needs to be, vanishing when it must, always tailored to fit the audience in front of her.

The Medical Record: *(Act 1, multiple scenes)*
A paper-and-ink witness whose memory is inconveniently perfect. It remembers what the Pink Script forgets.

The Pill Bottle: *(Act 1, multiple scenes)*
A silent accomplice and constant prop in the Usurper Queen's performance, a rattle of pills that whispers legitimacy to her illness claims.

The Wheelchair: *(Act 1, multiple scenes)*
Her most famous throne. A mobility aid weaponized into a visual shorthand for innocence, pity, and unquestioned victimhood.

The White Queen: *(Act 1, allegorical references)*
An occasional overseer of Wonderland's trials, all purity and poise, until you notice the frost in her judgments.

Tiger Lily: *(Act 1, allegorical references)*
A stubborn blossom in the Garden, refusing to bow to either the Usurper Queen or the Cult of the DeLuLus.

The Dormouse: *(Act 1, allegorical references)*
A minor but ever-present witness in the Court of the Painted Roses, sleepy-eyed but never truly unaware.

Index Act 1

The Hollow Root – p. 1, Prologue Beat 2
Mythic subterranean chamber beneath the Garden; womb of all potential records, breathing contradiction before narrative forms.

The Garden – p. 1, Prologue Beat 2
Allegorical realm of roots, witnesses, and invasive weeds; setting for truth and deception to entwine.

The Observance – p. 1, Prologue Beat 2
First Witness in the Hollow Root; hears the First Silence before any story is told.

The Silent Witnesses – p. 1, Prologue Beat 2
Keepers of the first and last truth; summoned when lies threaten the Garden's roots.

The Weeds – p. 2, Prologue Scene 6
Allegorical chorus; invasive truth-tellers rising where truth has been trampled.

Cult of the DeLuLus – p. 2, Prologue Beat 4
Faction dwelling in Rebrandingland; devoted to preserving and selling the Usurper Queen's narrative.

Rebrandingland – p. 2, Prologue Beat 4
Allegorical location where truth is traded like contraband.

Absinthe Rosemary Hightopp (The Hatter) – p. 3, Prologue Beat 4
Prosecutor in the Court of the Painted Roses; sharp-witted with concealed blades of truth.

Tisiphone Lysandra Chrysalis (The Caterpillar) – p. 3, Prologue Beat 4
Co-Counsel in the Court of the Painted Roses; coils and counsels with silken danger.

Tangie Amarantha Whiteviel (The White Rabbit) – p. 3, Prologue Beat 4
Narrative Archivist bridging the veil and Wonderland's shadow; carries truth between realms.

Judge Fidella Wrath – p. 3, Prologue Beat 4
Presiding authority of the Court of the Painted Roses; gavel as sharp as her judgment.

Petunia Verity Cawington – p. 3, Prologue Beat 4
One of the three black-feathered Witness sisters; speaks only when lies swell to breaking.

Ruby Begonia Cawington - p. 3, Prologue Beat 4
Witness sister; keeper of bitter truths.

Violet Darkly Cawington - p. 3, Prologue Beat 4
Witness sister; shadow-voiced recorder of deception.

Algorithms & Propaganda Plants - p. 3, Prologue Beat 4
Unnamed collective influencing narratives in allegorical realm.

Fancy Macelli - p. 4, Beat 5
Real-world prosecutor figure in forensic realm; co-author and investigator.

Amy Mackey - p. 4, Beat 5
Real-world investigator in forensic realm; co-author and analyst.

FOIA Records - p. 4, Beat 5
Primary forensic evidence source; includes court filings, medical documentation, and communications.

Gypsy Rose Blanchard - p. 7, Beat 7
Real figure at the center of forensic and allegorical narratives; cast in allegory as Gypmydia Verlaine Maris Crowley, the Usurper Queen.

Clauddine "Dee Dee" Blanchard - p. 7, Beat 7
Mother of Gypsy Rose; murder victim in forensic realm, reframed in allegorical trial.

Gypmydia Verlaine Maris Crowley (Usurper Queen) - p. 8, Beat 2 (Prologue Scene 6)
Allegorical identity of Gypsy Rose Blanchard; rose to power in the Glass Garden through performance and manipulation.

The Mourning Orchid - p. 8, Beat 2 (Prologue Scene 6)
Allegorical title for Clauddine Blanchard; symbolizing beauty cut down before second bloom.

Nick Godejohn - p. 8, Beat 2
Real-world co-defendant in Dee Dee Blanchard's murder; referenced as Nick's Victor in allegorical framing.

The Pink Script - p. 9, Beat 2
Symbolic manuscript and marketing weapon used by the Usurper Queen to reshape narrative.

The Victimhood Crown™ - p. 9, Beat 2
Marketed emblem of the Usurper Queen's status.

Microdeletion (1q21.1) - p. 9, Beat 2
Forensic medical fact suppressed in mainstream accounts to sustain alternate abuse narrative.

Brietta Slanderella Gasliette Von Objectionee - p. 10, Act 1 Scene 7
Editor-in-Chief of Pink-Script Publishing; allegorical lawyer to the Usurper Queen.

Widow Rue - p. 10, Act 1 Scene 7
Petunia Verity Cawington's allegorical role as curator of truths too bitter for sugar; rejects propaganda submissions.

Throne Fund - p. 10, Act 1 Scene 7
Cult of the DeLuLus' fundraising scheme for the Usurper Queen.

The Pink Standard - p. 11, Act 1 Scene 8
Propaganda publication of the Cult of the DeLuLus.

Cult of the DeLuLus (Rebuttal) - p. 16, Act 1 Scene 8
Faction defends the Usurper Queen after Widow Rue's rejection; equates editorial refusal to treason.

Crown of Thorns (symbolic) - p. 16, Act 1 Scene 8
Emblem of the Usurper Queen's self-styled persecution and martyrdom.

Stan Hancock - p. 18, Act 1 Scene 10
Lead detective in Dee Dee Blanchard's murder investigation; notes Gypsy's past-tense slip indicating knowledge of death.

The Past Tense - p. 18, Act 1 Scene 10
Allegorical embodiment of incriminating slips in language; betrays concealed truths.

Mike Stanfield - p. 19, Act 1 Scene 10
Real-world lawyer and manager to Gypsy Rose Blanchard; depicted as aiding in concealment of evidence and narrative rebranding.

Dr. Robert Steele - p. 20, Act 1 Scene 10
Neurologist; had access to Dee Dee's and Gypsy's Louisiana medical files despite later claims of lost records.

Dr. Bernardo Flasterstein - p. 20, Act 1 Scene 10
Pediatric neurologist who assessed Gypsy and raised suspicions; also had access to Louisiana medical history.

HBO (network) - p. 20, Act 1 Scene 10
Named in forensic context as aiding suppression of 1q21.1 diagnosis and shifting narrative toward Munchausen by Proxy framing.

There's a Story There – p. 21, Beat 6
Companion series concept; forensic short-form explorations of individual players.

Rod Blanchard – p. 22, Beat 7
Gypsy Rose's father; forensic accounts reveal inconsistencies between memoir claims and public record.

Kristy Blanchard – p. 22, Beat 7
Rod Blanchard's wife; appears in forensic context regarding family communications and housing records.

Rachel Callais – p. 24, Beat 7
Louisiana connection in forensic timeline; tied to Dee Dee's network prior to Missouri relocation.

Mike Callais – p. 24, Beat 7
Connected to Rachel Callais in Louisiana timeline; part of Dee Dee's earlier community circle.

Claudia Pitre – p. 24, Beat 7
Acquaintance in Louisiana chapter of Dee Dee's history; appears in relocation context.

Celeste Blanchard – p. 24, Beat 7
Relative in Blanchard family; mentioned in Louisiana backstory.

Jean Pierre Le Pichon – p. 25, Beat 7
Neurologist; appears in forensic documentation of medical oversight and diagnosis patterns.

Dr. Robert Bueckman – p. 25, Beat 7
Medical professional in timeline; appears in records cited for diagnosis cross-check.

Rachel Miller – p. 25, Beat 7
Forensic witness; appears in communications record and corroborative timeline evidence.

Ray Miller – p. 25, Beat 7
Connected to Rachel Miller; part of testimony context.

Aleah Woodmansee – p. 26, Beat 7
Friend of Gypsy Rose; recipient of text messages revealing 1q21.1 and murder plan with Nick Godejohn.

Jennifer Pan – p. 27, Beat 7
Referenced in allegorical commentary as another infamous case of filial violence.

Erin Caffey - p. 27, Beat 7
Included in comparative forensic context alongside Jennifer Pan and Diane Downs.

Diane Downs - p. 27, Beat 7
Comparative case reference for maternal harm dynamics.

Casey Anthony - p. 27, Beat 7
Referenced in forensic analysis for public narrative manipulation parallels.

Nick's Victor (mark) - p. 28, Beat 7
Signature "B" carved into Dee Dee's body in allegorical telling, marking Nick Godejohn's role.

Nick Godejohn - p. 31, Beat 7
Gypsy Rose's co-conspirator in Dee Dee Blanchard's murder; appears in both forensic records and allegorical narrative as a manipulated "Victor."

The Wheelchair - p. 32, Beat 8
Object character; symbol of Gypsy's performed illness and narrative captivity.

The Pill Bottle - p. 32, Beat 8
Object character; emblem of pharmaceutical manipulation and control.

The Medical Record - p. 32, Beat 8
Object character; in allegorical court, becomes a contested artifact wielded as both weapon and shield.

Absinthe Rosemary Hightopp - p. 34, Beat 8
Allegorical prosecutor; mirrors forensic role of confronting contradictions in Gypsy's narrative.

Tisiphone Lysandra Chrysalis - p. 34, Beat 8
Allegorical co-counsel; embodies metamorphosis of truth under cross-examination.

Judge Fidella Wrath - p. 34, Beat 8
Allegorical judge; enforces moral reckonings in the Court of the Painted Roses.

Petunia Verity Cawington - p. 34, Beat 8
First of the Silent Witness sisters; voice of clarity when lies grow uncontainable.

Ruby Begonia Cawington - p. 34, Beat 8
Second Silent Witness; allegorical custodian of inconvenient truths.

Violet Darkly Cawington - p. 34, Beat 8
Third Silent Witness; watches for the fatal bloom of deception.

Algorithms & Propaganda Plants – p. 34, Beat 8
Personified forces of misinformation within the allegorical court.

Widow Rue – p. 36, Beat 8
Curator of truths "too bitter for sugar"; rejects Cult of the DeLuLus' Pink-Script submission.

Brietta Slanderella Gasliette Von Objectionee – p. 36, Beat 8
Editor-in-chief and legal defender for the Usurper Queen; crafts PR under guise of justice.

Gypmydia Verlaine Maris Crowley – p. 36, Beat 8
Allegorical title for Gypsy Rose Blanchard; styled as the Usurper Queen in the fantasy realm.

The Pink Script – p. 36, Beat 8
Symbolic tool for narrative rebranding and monetization of victimhood.

Victimhood Crown™ – p. 36, Beat 8
Merchandised emblem of the Usurper Queen's self-fashioned martyrdom.

Throne Fund – p. 36, Beat 8
Cult of the DeLuLus' financial campaign to "restore" the Queen's place in her story.

Garden of Silent Witnesses – p. 38, Beat 9
Metaphorical sanctuary where truth is preserved until summoned.

The Weeds – p. 38, Beat 9
Collective allegorical narrators; thrive in neglected corners of truth's garden.

The Mourning Orchid / Cordelia Crowley – p. 39, Beat 9
Tragic royal figure within the allegorical world; her fate contrasts the Usurper Queen's rise.

Marigold Finch Tinch – p. 42, Beat 10
Allegorical character; appears in garden sequences as a quiet keeper of overlooked truths.

Ravena Sage – p. 43, Beat 10
Allegorical witness; embodies foresight and patient observation.

Hoxie Serenity LeRue – p. 44, Beat 10
Allegorical figure tied to rural lore within the fantasy court.

Appendix X: The Registry of Shadows & Statements

Filed by: Court Archivist of the Painted Roses
Filed under: Cross-Referenced Identities, Allegorical Realms, Forensic Evidence Trail

Bailiff Clovis Brickhouse - p. 27
Allegorical bailiff of the Court of the Painted Roses; towering, immovable, a stone wall with a badge. His silence weighs more than his voice.

Beckerman, Dr. Robert - p. 52
Real-world doctor cited in medical file discussions, connected to the disputed record of diagnoses.

Blanchard, Aleah Woodmansee - p. 72
Friend of Gypsy Rose Blanchard; received confessional texts about Nick Godejohn and the 1q21.1 diagnosis, acting as both confidant and reluctant witness.

Blanchard, Clauddine "Dee Dee" - pp. 17, 21, 24
Mother of Gypsy Rose Blanchard; presented in real-world trial materials and reframed in allegorical testimony as the Mourning Orchid's guardian before betrayal.

Blanchard, Gypsy Rose - pp. 14, 17, 23
Central figure in both forensic and allegorical realms; convicted in the real-world murder of her mother. See also: *Crowley, Gypmydia Verlaine Maris*.

Blanchard, Kristy - p. 45
Relative of Gypsy Rose, referenced in the forensic reconstruction of family dynamics.

Blanchard, Rod - p. 30
Real father of Gypsy Rose Blanchard; appears in forensic segments as a witness and in allegorical realm as a sideline king avoiding the throne.

Body Mapping Revenge 🔖 - p. 29
Bone Shard Glossary term: the symbolic use of physical harm or markings to communicate intent or leave a signature in a crime.

Callais, Mike - p. 32
Real-world figure tied to the extended Blanchard family network; appears in forensic timeline. Helped get the Habitat House for Dee Dee. Accused Dee Dee of poisoning his mother. Friend of Kristy.

Callais, Rachel - p. 32
Real-world figure; mentioned in family and witness context in Act 1. Married to Mike Callais. Pitre relation by birth.

Cain, Detective Jasper Ransom - p. 28
Allegorical investigator whose name drips with the promise of ransom and the price of truth; shadow to Detective Hancock in the allegorical realm.

Cawington, Petunia Verity - pp. 9, 14
One of the three black-feathered Witness sisters; speaks only when lies threaten to burst the realm apart. See also: *Silent Witnesses* 🌿.

Cawington, Ruby Begonia - pp. 9, 14, 36
One of the three Silent Witness sisters; red-feathered, sharp-eyed, keeper of unspoken verdicts.

Cawington, Violet Darkly - pp. 9, 14
One of the three black-feathered Witness sisters; embodies foreboding silence.

Chrysalis, Tisiphone Lysandra - pp. 9, 14
Allegorical Co-Counsel (The Caterpillar) whose parasitic coil suggests quiet manipulation behind the Queen's defense.

Court Reporter - p. 27
Unnamed allegorical scribe in the Court of the Painted Roses; captures every word, though not all will survive the Queen's edits.

Crowley, Cordelia (The Mourning Orchid) - pp. 17, 21
Allegorical victim archetype whose bloom was cut before full flower; tied to the fall of the Garden. See also: *Mourning Orchid*.

Crowley, Gypmydia Verlaine Maris - pp. 14, 17, 23
Allegorical embodiment of Gypsy Rose Blanchard; styled as the "Usurper Queen" in the Court of the Painted Roses; crowned in pity, wrapped in the Pink Script. See also: *Blanchard, Gypsy Rose*.

Cult of the DeLuLus 🌿 - pp. 14, 18
Garden Vine term for the Queen's most devoted followers; devoted to narrative maintenance through denial, amplification, and merchandised loyalty.

Dormouse - p. 35
Allegorical object/character; dream-frayed and quietly listening, a recurring figure in Garden metaphors of inattention and willful blindness.

Flasterstein, Dr. Bernardo - p. 22
Neurologist who evaluated Gypsy Rose Blanchard; real-world figure tied to the contested timeline of medical evidence.

FOIA Request #225-078 - pp. 40-46
Public records confirming medical file availability and relocation records; used to disprove trial claims of missing documentation post-Katrina.

Garden of Silent Witnesses 🌿 - pp. 9, 16
Metaphorical realm where truth is kept alive beneath allegorical soil; only awakened when lies grow large enough to strangle the Garden.

Gypmydia's Narrative 🌿 - p. 34
Object/Concept character; the evolving Pink Script version of the Queen's own myth, replacing earlier accounts for marketable effect.

Hancock, Detective Stan - p. 24
Lead detective in the investigation of Dee Dee Blanchard's murder; noted for detecting Gypsy's past-tense slip during interrogation.

Hearspray, Vonda Lynn - p. 28
Allegorical courtroom observer; gossip as currency, spraying half-truths like perfume.

Hightopp, Absinthe Rosemary - pp. 8, 13
Prosecutor in the Court of the Painted Roses; allegorical stand-in for strategic confrontation and hat-brimmed subtext. Wields arguments like concealed blades.

Hightopp, Absinthe Rosemary - See: *Absinthe Rosemary Hightopp.*

Learned Helplessness 🦴 - p. 33
Bone Shard Glossary term: state in which repeated adversity teaches inaction, regardless of actual options for escape.

Le Pichon, Dr. Jean Pierre - p. 48
Physician involved in assessments of Gypsy Rose Blanchard; positioned in the contested record of medical oversight.

Lunetta "Lunk" Skeemington - p. 28
Allegorical character whose plotting is as blunt as her nickname; often seen perched at the back of the courtroom.

Medical Record - p. 34
Object/Concept character; in forensic realm, literal chart of diagnoses and history; in allegorical Garden, a root-bound ledger of truths the Queen wishes uprooted.

Memory Laundering 🦴 - p. 35
Bone Shard Glossary term: altering or re-contextualizing memories to remove damaging implications.

Miller, Rachel - p. 21
Real-world associate who is listed as one of the proxies on Gypsy's POA

Miller, Ray - p. 21
Real-world associate who is listed as one of the proxies on Gypsy's POA; connected to Rachel Miller in narrative placement.

Myth Maintenance 🦴 - p. 36
Bone Shard Glossary term: sustaining a false narrative via repetition, selective sourcing, and audience targeting.

Narrative Pivot Delay 🦴 - p. 20
Bone Shard Glossary term: intentional postponement of key narrative shifts to control audience reaction or adapt to new evidence.

Narrative Restitution 🦴 - p. 28
Bone Shard Glossary term: reclaiming a narrative to restore perceived ownership or moral high ground.

Narrative Self-Enhancement 🦴 - p. 37
Bone Shard Glossary term: amplifying one's role in a story for self-promotion or image control.

Nick Godejohn - pp. 55, 61
Accomplice and boyfriend of Gypsy Rose Blanchard; participated in Dee Dee Blanchard's murder.

Objection Von, Brietta Slanderella Gasliette - pp. 14, 18
Allegorical lawyer/editor for the Usurper Queen; voice of the Cult of the DeLuLus in the Pink Script Publishing promotions.

Past-Tense Slip (Psychological Marker) - p. 24
Forensic psychology concept: unintentional use of past tense betrays hidden knowledge (e.g., Gypsy saying "I loved my mom" during interrogation).

Pill Bottle - p. 34
Object/Concept character; forensic evidence and allegorical seed-pod of dependency, control, and poison.

Pink Script 🌿 - pp. 14, 17, 18
Allegorical document and publishing brand wielded as narrative weaponry; merges merchandising with myth-making.

Pitre, Claudia - p. 33
Real-world contact linked to family communications in the reconstructed timeline.

Professor Butterella Snortlebottom - p. 28
Allegorical academic, expert in absurdities, frequently summoned to "explain" the unexplainable in court.

Retcon 🦴 - p. 20
Bone Shard Glossary term: rewriting or ignoring previously established facts to benefit a new version of a narrative.

Rue, Widow - pp. 14, 18
Allegorical curator of truths "too bitter for sugar"; gatekeeper who rejects propaganda pieces from the Cult of the DeLuLus.

Silent Witnesses 🌿 - pp. 9, 16
Allegorical keepers of the first and last truth; intervene only when the Garden's survival is at stake.

Skreachington, Lunetta "Lunk" - p. 28
Allegorical character whose plotting is as blunt as her nickname; often seen perched at the back of the courtroom.

Social Role Enforcement 🦴 - p. 37
Bone Shard Glossary term: societal pressure to act in ways that conform to a pre-assigned identity.

Stanfield, Mike - p. 21
Real-world lawyer and manager for Gypsy Rose Blanchard; tied to public narrative shaping and post-trial positioning.

Strategic Humiliation 🦴 - p. 37
Bone Shard Glossary term: targeted use of embarrassment or degradation to gain psychological or narrative advantage.

Tiger Lily - p. 35
Object/Concept character; blooms in moments of narrative bloodletting, petals stained with implication.

Usurper Queen 🌿 - pp. 14, 17, 23
Garden Vine epithet for Gypmydia Verlaine Maris Crowley; title framing her ascension via deception and performance.

Violet Darkly Cawington - pp. 9, 14
One of the three black-feathered Witness sisters; embodies foreboding silence.

Wheelchair - p. 34
Object/Concept character; both real-world mobility device and allegorical throne of sympathy from which the Queen ruled her early narrative.

Whiteveil, Tangie Amarantha - pp. 9, 14, 20
Narrative Archivist and allegorical embodiment of the White Rabbit; carries truth between the veil and Wonderland's shadow. See also: *White Rabbit; Silent Witnesses* 🌿.

Witnesses (Three Black-Feathered Sisters) 🌿 - pp. 9, 14
Petunia Verity, Ruby Begonia, and Violet Darkly Cawington; allegorical observers who speak only when the realm's lies are too large to contain.

Wrath, Judge Fidella Eternity - pp. 9, 14
Allegorical judge of the Court of the Painted Roses; gavel as capable of breaking bone as wood.

Wretched Jr., Hobart Gaveldozer - p. 27
Allegorical caricature of heavy-handed legal authority; clears the court with a glance and a gavel-slam.

Preview Cawing Out the Truth Act 2- Coming Sept. 2025

Act 2: The Rebranding of a Corpse

Filed under: Strategic Humiliation, Memory Laundering, and the Murder of Reputation

- 📘 **Rebutting:** *My Time to Stand*, Chapter 2 - "Cajun"
- 🎧 **Companion Podcast:** *Gathering of the Crows*
- 🪶 **Garden Broadcast:** Broadcast 4 - "Checkmate in Progress"
- 🎙 **Filed by:** Miss Petunia Verity Cawington
- 🗃 **Filed Under:** Narrative Necromancy, Weaponized Memory, Misapplied Mythology
- ⚖ **Lead Prosecutor:** Fancy Macelli
- 🧠 **Narrative Analyst:** Mack

Act 2: Scene 1: The Corpse Was Convicted

📁 *Filed under: Posthumous Trials, Pretty Lies, and the Criminalization of the Dead*

"They couldn't convict her mother in life,
so they sentenced her memory to death."
- The Garden Wire Archives

This is the part where the glitter gets weaponized.

In Chapter Two of *My Time to Stand*, Gypsy Rose does not simply recall the past, she rewrites it. Not as memoir, but as mitigation. The girl with the curled lashes and soft voice is not recounting trauma. She is building a defense.

Dee Dee Blanchard, already silenced in life and slaughtered in death, is stripped further of her dignity here transformed into a clown, a compulsive liar, a sad fat woman who drank vinegar and told teenage lies about rockstars. The aim is erosion, not remembrance.

She is not just stripping away these moments from her mother. She is stripping away the memories her friends had. She is stripping anyone who lived at times memories and trivializing the things we loved. The time was different, and we cherished things. Who are you to judge?

Why do you take any chance you can to destroy any goodness, happiness for a woman you used to call you "best friend." Even now that the world knows what she was doing was guarding your life you said right?

She was with every doctor who tried to help you and did, she gave you amazing trips, she gave up everything to make your life incredible because she honestly thought you may not make it. She is why you are not BLIND today. You insult every person ever in your life.

This act examines that erosion.
The choice of insults.
The pacing of reveals.
The manipulative cadence of performative innocence.

From pageant queen to punchline.
From teen romance to retroactive grooming charge.
From mother to monster.

But here, in *Cawing Out the Truth*, we stop the narrative spin.

This is where we unmask the myths and the truth claws its way out from under the tiara.

Let the record reflect:
The corpse was crowned by critics, not mourners.

But Gypsy did not build this mythology alone. She had help.
From the sidelines stepped a father rebranded.
The man who watched from afar now walks beside her, not as witness, but as co-author

Let the proceedings begin.

🎭 Act 2, Scene 3: The March of Microaggressions

SECTION HEADER: 🖊 Narrative Setup – Memoir as Ammunition
SUMMARY BLURB: Before the courtroom opens, the smearing begins.
FILED BY: The Garden Wire Archives
FILED UNDER: Narrative Intent – Psychological Framing – Weaponized Recollection
REALM: Narrative Courtroom & Memoir Dissection

💼 Beat 1 ~ The Tone of a Weapon

Before we examine courtroom facts, before we dissect the contradictions, we need to understand the *tone* this memoir sets, not just in content, but in strategy.
Because *My Time to Stand* is not a recounting. It is a weapon.
And Chapter Two does not begin with grief.
It begins with a gavel of shame.

Gypsy does not mourn her mother.
She mocks her.
Not with facts and with *fragments*.

This is not evidence.
It is humiliation by anecdote.

So, let's step into Exhibit D.
Not to argue yet.
But to listen. To read. To document.
Because before rebuttal comes recognition.

What follows is not commentary.
It's just the quotes.
And the quiet sound of a crown being shattered.

🏷 Beat 2 ~ Strategic Humiliation

Exhibit D – The Smear Parade Begins

Before the courtroom opens and the witnesses are called, let's look at what Gypsy Rose Blanchard does in the *first few paragraphs* of Chapter 2 of *My Time to Stand*.

She does not recall.
She *ridicules*.

She does not build a case.
She launches a smear campaign.

So, let's roll the tape, no commentary, no rebuttal yet.
Just the quotes. Just the strategy.
This is not memoir.
This is premeditated degradation.

💧 The rapid-fire begins:

🎭 *Beat 3 ~ The Petty Parade: Confetti Bombs & Character Assassinations*

📌 **"Her birth surname was Pitre, which means 'clown' in French."**
Gypsy opens the chapter by mocking her mother's *literal name.* The goal? Turn Dee Dee into a joke before the reader even meets her.

📌 **"Some people pronounce it 'Pet-tree,' like the dish where penicillin was discovered."**
This is not wit, it is *symbolic contamination.* A name becomes a bacteria joke. And a woman becomes an infection.

📌 **"She was twenty-three. She told my dad she was twenty-one."**
Instant implication of deceit. Framed to sound like seduction, not survival. Dee Dee becomes a predator with a fake ID.

📌 **"She had a picture with a rockstar and told everyone she was dating him."**
A teenager's moment of excitement reframed as pathological delusion.

📌 **"She was ROTC Queen in 1986... but that wasn't really anything."**
A rare achievement dismissed. One ribbon, one crown, one memory smeared into meaninglessness.

📌 **"She had eating disorders and body issues... but also control issues."**
Vulnerability transformed into volatility. Her pain is not understood; it is used to foreshadow madness.

📌 **"She drank vinegar to be beautiful."**
Because nothing says mental illness like vintage weight loss folklore stripped of all compassion.

📌 **"They had sex three times. That's all."**
Unverified bedroom tallies. Gypsy turns speculation into scripture.

📌 **"Maybe she always hated men."**
Ah yes, the final flourish. Not just desperate. Not just unstable. A man-hating, sexually manipulative, grotesquely bitter caricature.

𝒞𝓁𝑜𝓈𝒾𝓃𝑔 𝒜𝓃𝓃𝑜𝓉𝒶𝓉𝒾𝑜𝓃: 🗒️ *𝒩𝑒𝓍𝓉 𝒩𝑜𝓉𝑒*

"She does not describe her mother's crimes.
She constructs them out of gossip, shame, and old photos."

- 📎 *End of Parade. Begin the cross-examinations.*
- 📄 Proceed to: 📁 *Chapter Docket 2 – The People v. The Confused Crown*

⚖️ Act 2, Scene 4: The People v. Gypsy Rose Blanchard

Filed Within: *Defamation Docket: The Mock Trial*
Tethered To: *Narrative Mirror: Act 2, Scene 3 – The March of Microaggressions*
Reflected In: *Court of Public Opinion – Mirror Segment: Strategic Humiliation*
Lead Prosecutor: Fancy Macelli
Narrative Analyst: Amy Mackey
Filed Under: Character Defamation - Narrative Manipulation - Myth as Motive
Exhibit in Review: Chapter Two of *My Time to Stand*
Scene Type: 📁 Evidentiary Presentation – Jury Examination

🎙️ Beat 1 ~ Court in Session: Chapter Docket 2

1. The Autopsy of a Mother's Reputation

The gavel drops once. The courtroom falls silent. Across the aisle, mirrors flicker in the Court of Public Opinion. The jury of record and the garden specters lean in as the next exhibit begins.

ABSINTHE ROSEMARY HIGHTOPP (PROSECUTION):
Members of the jury,
what you are about to hear is not sworn testimony.
It was not delivered under oath.
It was not cross-examined, fact-checked, or subjected to discovery.

No, what you are about to hear was *published*.
Marketed. Monetized.
Filed under the genre of memoir but constructed like a myth.

We submit to this court that Chapter Two of *My Time to Stand* is not a remembrance.
It is a rewrite.
A carefully styled alibi in hardcover form strategically designed to recast guilt as grief and self-preservation as moral license.

The defense calls this healing.
We call it *narrative laundering*.

And here, under the scrutiny of this court, we return the record to clarity.
This chapter is not a cry for help.
It is an *execution of character*.

Gypsy Rose Blanchard does not defend herself in this chapter.
She *destroys her mother.*
Not with evidence.
But with insinuation, mockery, and performative regret.

No citations.
No records.
No charges filed during her mother's life.
Only a parade of petty jabs and vintage rumors, sewn together with just enough vulnerability to pass for truth.

With the court's permission, the prosecution now enters evidence:

🎬 Beat 2 ~ 📄 Exhibit D2: "Cajun Confessional: Memoir or Motive

Chapter 2: Cajun" from My Time to Stand

Filed By: Lead Prosecutor Fancy Macelli
Co-Counsel: Amy Mackey, Narrative Analyst
Origin Source: *My Time to Stand*, Chapter Two, by Gypsy Rose Blanchard
Referenced In:

- Narrative: *Act 2, Scene 3, Beat 3 – The Petty Parade: Confetti Bombs & Character Assassinations*
- Garden Court Broadcast: *Strategic Humiliation*

📒 **Purpose:**

To enter evidence a literary artifact weaponized as post-mortem character assassination. The defense may claim memoir. The prosecution asserts myth making and defamation.

📄 **Filed Under:**

- Character Defamation
- Narrative Manipulation
- Myth as Motive
- Posthumous Reputation Sabotage

📎 **Contextual Linkage:**

This excerpt serves as the primary forensic artifact in the prosecution's claim that Chapter Two of *My Time to Stand* does not serve as healing or reflection, but as a calculated smear campaign against the deceased mother of the defendant.

FANCY (CONTINUED):

Before we present commentary, before rebuttal, before analysis;
Let the record show what she chose to say.
Let the jury hear, unedited, the first wave of her attack.

We ask the court to listen not only to the words,
But to the timing, the choice, and the intention.

This is not memoir.
This is *strategic humiliation*.

The prosecution now tenders the following passages as verbatim excerpts from Chapter Two.

Let the record show:
The corpse was convicted posthumously.
Not by a jury of peers,
But by a daughter with a publishing deal.

In Chapter Two, the defendant begins her real work, not in survival, but in **sanitized defamation**.

She reshapes her mother into a grotesque caricature:
A woman so *frumpy*, so *delusional*, so *pitiful* that her murder feels like mercy.

She mocks her appearance.
She questions her virginity.
She recounts every rumor, every slight, every insecurity, not as memory, but as justification.

And yet...
Not one claim is supported by medical records, no accusation is backed by law enforcement.
and there are no charges substantiated by court proceedings.

Your Honor, Members of the Jury,
what we place before you today are not grief on paper.

It is strategy.
This exhibit is not memoir.
It is narrative warfare.

The defendant's chapter does not open with mourning.
It opens with mockery.
Her mother, Clauddinnea, "Dee Dee" Blanchard, is not humanized.
She is caricatured.
Humiliated.
Reduced.

Let the record show:
Gypsy Rose Blanchard did not just kill her mother's body.
She sentenced her reputation to death, posthumously, in print.

⚖️ *Beat 3 ~ Death by Anecdote: A Eulogy of the Mutilated Memory in Reverse*

Filed Under: Posthumous Defamation - Weaponized Nostalgia - Strategic Memoir
Realm: 👨‍⚖️ Mock Trial — The Defamation Docket
Mirrored In: 💐 *Court of Public Opinion — The Petty Parade: Confetti Bombs & Character Assassinations*
Referenced Exhibit: 📄 *Exhibit D - Chapter Two: "Cajun" from My Time to Stand*

Summary Blurb:
The prosecution turns its full attention to the carefully curated insults in Chapter Two of Gypsy Rose Blanchard's memoir. Rather than mourning her mother, she dissects her one anecdote at a time.

What begins as memoir soon becomes motive, crafted to erode sympathy for the dead and soften the public's moral recoil. From weight jokes to speculative virginity shaming, Gypsy builds her own defense not in court, but in narrative.

This is not a recollection, it is a eulogy in reverse. And it stinks of strategy.

📄 Act 2, Scene 5: Exhibit D - Cajun Confessional: Memoir or Motive

Excerpts from Chapter 2 "My Time to Stand"

Beat 1 ~ On Her Mother's Appearance and Insecurities:

"By the time my mother was twelve, she had gained a lot of weight. According to her, she 'blew up,' and she tried to wrap her middle in cellophane to sweat off the fat."
"Apparently, my grandmother Emma body-shamed Mama relentlessly, calling her fat."
"Mama began a very unhealthy diet and soon developed anorexia and bulimia."

Beat 2 ~ On Her Mother's Claims and Embellishments:

"She claimed she was in a relationship with Jack Russell, the lead singer of the eighties hair band Great White."
"She told anyone who saw it [a framed photo] that Jack had mailed the photo to her because they were in a relationship, which was completely false."
"Sometimes she sent flowers to herself and told people they were from various rock stars. With lies, she created lore."

Fact Check:
This story references Jackie Blades from *Night Ranger*, not Jack Russell of *Great White*. Dee Dee's friend Suzette confirmed this was a long-standing exaggeration involving a fan photo.

Beat 3 ~ On Virginity:

"Mama also claimed she was a virgin before she met my dad. I'm not about to ask my dad his opinion on this. But I know that being a groupie and a virgin cannot be true at the same time."

Additional Context:
In a recent public panel, Kristy Blanchard reinforced this shaming narrative. She claimed Dee Dee once bragged that *Great White* thanked her in their liner notes. Kristy's response:

"For what? All the time she spent on her knees?"

This is not a memoir; rather, it stands for generational adversity presented under the guise of character development.

 Beat 4 ~ On Dee Dee's Pageant Claims:

"She made it seem that after that crowning [ROTC queen], she had been entered into pageants all around the state, except that wasn't true."
"I have come to find out that she attended pageants out of the obligation of being the 1986 ROTC queen. She had not been entered in any pageants after that."

 Beat 5 ~ On Feelings of Bitterness and Projection:

"She often made it a point to remind me that she could've been that somebody if she hadn't given it all up to take care of me."
"She used to drink vinegar to make her skin snow white, so she'd be more beautiful."
"It almost seemed like she was trying to make me feel even smaller, in my wheelchair, with no teeth, malnourished, androgynous, with no attractiveness at all, most of the time dressed as a boy."

 Beat 6 ~ On Her Mother's Narrative Control:

"I think when you love to tell stories, like she did, you learn early on to choose your words and their delivery with precision, the better to ensnare the listener."
"With lies, she created lore. She was always telling stories. That was just Dee Dee."

FANCY (CONT'D):
Your Honor, these are not neutral recollections.
They are **strategic reframing** designed to erode sympathy for a murder victim.
In this courtroom, the dead cannot take the stand.
So, it is our duty to ensure they are not buried a second time by narrative.

Her mother is not mourned.
She is **mocked.**

"She created lore." But the truth is simple:
Claudinnea "Dee Dee" Blanchard **was a real woman.**
And this book, the one that claims to tell her daughter's truth, rewrites her life to justify her death.

◆ Let the record reflect:
We do not intend to bury Gypsy Rose Blanchard with this case.
We intend to **exhume the truth** she paved over.

🎙 *Beat 7 ~ Exhibit D Admitted into Evidence.*

🎙 *America's Sweetheart Murderers* - Chapter Two Segment
🎧 *Gathering of the Crows*, Episode 2 Companion

The prosecution is ready.
And Dee Dee Blanchard is finally being heard.

[JUDGE nods solemnly.]
JUDGE: Exhibit D is accepted into evidence. Proceed with caution, counsel. The line between truth and theatrics grows thin.
FANCY: Understood, Your Honor.

JURY FOREPERSON (softly, to another juror):
She doesn't just tell stories.
She rewrites history.

www.ingramcontent.com/pod-product-compliance
Lightning Source LLC
Chambersburg PA
CBHW080540030426
42337CB00024B/4805